Mythos and Logos
of
The Warlis

CASTES AND TRIBES OF INDIA-SERIES

1. Continuity and Change Among the Ahom/ **Nitul Kumar Gogai**
2. Ethnography of a Nomadic Tribe: A Study of Yanadi/ **N. Sudhakar Rao**
3. Mythos and Logos of the Warlis: A Tribal World View/ **Ajay Dandekar (Ed.)**
4. Naga Cultural Attires and Musical Instruments/ **A. Lanu Ao (Ed.)**
5. Socio-Cultural Study of Scheduled Tribes: The Pardhans of Maharashtra/ **S.R. Murkute**
6. The Banjara/ **S.G. Deogaonkar** and **Shailaja S. Deogaonkar**
7. The Kolam Tribals/ **S.G. Deogaonkar** and **Leena Deogaonkar Baxi**
8. The Korku Tribals/ **S.G. Deogaonkar** and **Shailaja S. Deogaonkar**
9. Tribal Dance and Songs/ **S.G. Deogaonkar** and **Shailaja S. Deogaonkar**

The Compiler

Fr. Avellino Remedios has spent most of his life with the Warlis of the Thane district. First as a Jesuit seminarian and now as a priest he shares a special relationship with the Warlis. He brings a lifetime of experience to his work.

The Editor

Dr. Ajay Dandekar did his doctorate from the Centre for Historical Studies, Jawaharlal Nehru University in the early nineties. Since then he has been associated with the IGNCA and later a lecturer at Deccan College. His primary interests are with the pastoralists and hunter-gatherers of western India. He is now a Senior Research Fellow at the Social Science Centre, Mumbai, and a trustee of the Gunter Sonteimer foundation, Pune.

The Social Science Centre

This is a research centre started in 1980 on the campus of St. Xavier's College, Mumbai. Its focus has been on action-oriented participatory studies on issues of social relevance and it works closely with voluntary agencies and NGOs in the field. The Centre's publications have covered various issues of identity and culture, education and development, and other related fields of research. Dr. Rudolf C. Heredia received his doctorate from the University of Chicago in 1979. He is the founder director of the Centre. His present interests include affirmative action in comparative perspective and 'eco-communities' in wasteland zones of western Maharashtra.

Castes and Tribes of India Series-4

MYTHOS AND LOGOS OF THE WARLIS
A Tribal Worldview

Compiled by
AVELLINO REMEDIOS

Edited by
AJAY DANDEKAR

Foreword by
RUDOLF C. HEREDIA

CONCEPT PUBLISHING COMPANY PVT. LTD.
NEW DELHI-110059

ISBN: 978-81-7022-692-5

Edition 2025

Published and Printed by

Concept
Since 1974

Concept Publishing Company Pvt. Ltd.
A/15-16, Commercial Block, Mohan Garden,
New Delhi-110059 (India)
T : 91-11-41101460
E : publishing@conceptpub.com, *W*: www.conceptpub.com

FOREWORD

THE WARLIS

The People and their History

The Warli tribals are located mostly in the hilly tracts along the West coast in northern Maharashtra and southern Gujarat. This ethnographic study was made in Thane district where their largest numbers are found. However they are also scattered through the adjacent areas, though in much smaller numbers. In Thane district, out of a total tribal population of 7,29,424 they constitute 3,23,791, with concentrations mainly in Talasari, Dahanu, Palaghar and Jawhar talukas. Some of the other tribes in the district are the Thakurs, Kathkaris and the Mahadeva Kolis. Clearly the Warlis are the dominant tribal group here. According to the 1991 Census the total tribal percentage of Thane district stands at 18.21, which indicates a fall figure of 1981, which was 21.76 percent.

However, the tribals have not been not been able to protect themselves, or to assert their human rights, or preserve their indigenous culture. Both their cultural identity and human dignity have been under threat from the outsider, here as elsewhere.

Already in 1936 the Symington Report on the Aboriginal Hill Tribes of the Partially Excluded Areas in the Province of Bombay records how their lives were "wretched in the extreme and constitute a blot on the administration" (Report 1939). Rack renting, forced labour or vetu, and widespread indebtedness were rampant. The progressive alienation of tribal lands in the area began with the Portuguese occupation, intensified under the Marathas and culminated with the British. The colonial system with its monetised economy as opposed to barter, and legalised rights, as opposed to traditional and community ones, left the tribals even more vulnerable to exploitation and oppression. In spite of the apparent protection given to them by the new government after Independence, the deterioration in their life situation has only been further accentuated in post-colonial India.

For, their tribal culture was not able to cope with the changes consequent on the model of development now adopted. Neither could they protect themselves from its adverse effects. The result has been a progressive withdrawal of the tribals over decades into more remote areas, where the forest could still be their provider and protector. But as these areas too are drawn more and more into the process of change and modernisation, there is less and less space for the tribals and their way of life.

The government policy of "integration not assimilation" is intended to leave an autonomous cultural space for our tribals, while bringing them into the political economy of the mainstream. But such a policy has been problematic in its conceptualisation and more so its implementation. To our mind it has left much to be desired in its impact on tribal identity and dignity. The "Adivasi Revolt" of 1940s led by the then Communist Party of India under Godavari Parulekar, brought into prominence, "The Story of the Warli Peasants : In Struggle." (Parulekar 1975). But the Communists have focused mainly on economic issues. The Congress with Thakkarbapa, and other non-government agencies in the area have tried to address social concerns like education (Naik 1978). However, it is only with the Kashtakari Sangathana, a Marxist-Leninist group, that the cultural identity of the tribals is being given some serious attention in the political arena.

The Jesuits and their Endeavor

The Jesuit contribution to the study of "mission lands" has been significant and multifaceted. India was one of their earliest adventures. They introduced the first movable-type printing press in Goa in the sixteenth Century. They published "a variety of grammars and guides to vernacular languages" (Boxer 1969 : 348). Father Thomas Stephen, an English Jesuit was the one of the first to see the connection, between Indian and European languages. (Carpentier 1933 : iv) In fact, some scholars who are quite critical of the Jesuit mission, could be embarrassingly lavish in their praise of Jesuit missionaries:

> "It may be safely asserted that the modern knowledge of geography of the then unknown parts of the world and the acquaintance with the history, religions and social customs of Asiatic, African and American people and races has been founded by the Jesuit missionaries". (Ibid xxxvii)

Indeed, it was in this encounter with the cultures and peoples of the mission lands that the Jesuits made their best contribution to a deeper dialogue and some would add, made some of their worst mistakes as well. Without doubt much of the missionary endeavor represented an aggressive inroad into the culture and religion of the indigenous people, which left behind a trail of ruin. But there were at least some among the Jesuits who did attempt a more sympathetic dialogue with, and a more genuine adaptation to these people.

Fr. Avellino Remedios belongs very much to this Jesuit tradition of dialogue and inculturation. This has indeed been the inspiration of his work with the Warlis. His first encounters with them were as a boy growing up in Vasai, one of the more developed talukas of Thane district in the 1930's and 40's. Here the Warlis were out of their milieu, alienated from their natural habitat, and at the bottom of the social ladder. Mostly they worked as bonded laborers. But already then they did arouse his empathy and curiosity.

Later as a Jesuit seminarian in Talasari and then as a priest there, his encounters with them moved him deeply. There seemed to be a certain primeval innocence here that was being violated and the mission with their altruistic intentions of religious conversion and social upliftment seemed unable to reach these people because they had not really understood them. It was this quest that inspired Fr. Remedios in his venture to understand in order to be understood. But he soon discovered that in trying to reach the Warlis, he arrived at a better self-understanding of his own cultural boundaries and religious horizons.

He soon realized that the mission had neglected to consider the cultural context in their interventions with these people. Of the many endeavors on their behalf few came close to attaining the intended goals: religious liberation from the tyranny of their belief in evil spirits, social development through cooperatives and improved agriculture, formal education to improve their life chances in the changing world around them, access to curative and preventative medical aid to preserve and improve their health, etc.. Some of these efforts were put through with much self-sacrifice and even heroism.

However, too much of this was culturally alien to, as well as alienating for these tribals. Mission work was out of phase with the rhythms of the people's lives. But if the mission's efforts were frustrating for the missionaries, in no small measure was the loss that of the tribals as well. For the market mentality and non-tribal culture pressing in from the outside on them now seems poised to undermine both their identity and dignity, leaving the tribals worse off than ever before. Those among them who managed to cope, have now formed a better off class, an elite of kinds that have claimed for themselves the opportunities meant for all.

Fr. Remedios's response to this situation was to enter into the cultural world of the Warli and describe it from within. Any response to their crisis would have to be from within their culture, not from without, by an affirmation, not a negation of it. An outsider could but be a catalyst in this process. To prepare for this role, Fr. Remedios began to record and describe the culture he encountered. This was a labor of love over many years, and it is now being shared with a wider audience in the hope that they too will be enriched by the encounter.

The Study its Relevance

This collection began as one person's venture over many years to describe a part of that culture before it is lost in an ethnocide, which seems ever more likely to happen to tribal peoples here as elsewhere today. But first it had to be critically reviewed verified and audited for a larger reading public. This has been undertaken very ably and painstaking by Dr. Ajay Dandekar, who has been working in collaboration with Fr. Remedios for some years now. Their presentation here is very much a joint effort.

Dr. Dandekar was just the person to bring intellectual rigour and academic credibility to this collection, for he is a qualified ethnographer with wide experiences in the field, especially in Maharashtra. The scholar and priest have brought together head and heart, with a commitment to, and an empathy for the Warlis which is convincingly manifested in this text.

The last published Study of The Warlis was by K. J. Sauve in 1945, based on his doctoral dissertation which would need some updating today. A more popular study in Marathi appeared in 1955 which romaticises the Warli as the "Jungle cha Raja" (King of the Jungle). Warli art was popularised in the 1970s and has become almost the norm for tribal art in this country. Yashodhara Dalmia has discussed aspects of Warli painting, but it was more an aesthetic presentation than an ethnographic study of the tribals.

However, this monograph takes a different and hopefully more relevant approach. It is not directed at critiquing government policy. Rather, it is concerned with tribal culture and is addressed to those involved with these tribals. It could be used to sensitise policy makers closer to the ground, as well as to affirm those for whom this policy is made. Certainly, we hope it will have an interest for academics and scholars, but primarily it is meant more for the Warlis themselves and those in solidarity with them in their struggles. Indeed, we do want to reach beyond the Warlis as well. For what happens to them is but part of the same process affecting other tribals in different parts of our world.

This is not the best place for a long discussion on the politics of ethnography. Given the limited space we have, rather than digressing into that discourse, we will here locate this study within it. Our option here is not for some objectivist neutrality of the ivory tower, nor in the ethical relativism of postmodern multiplicity, but in a commitment to tribal identity and their right to culture, to tribal dignity and their right to equality.

For we believe that our tribals have a contribution to make, and a challenge to pose to us. For the tribal is the "other" who questions and critiques our society in ways that cannot be ignored, if indeed, we want to address the fundamental issues of our development within a humanist agenda, issues of social equity, ecological sustainability, people's participation, cultural autonomy, and democratic integration; issues that must concern us all because they touch us all, less and less gently with the accumulating crises of our society.

This study has been a very long time in gestation. The earliest collection of this material goes back many decades. It has been continuously updated over the years. Here it is presented to the reader in a coherent and accessible form. Many have already used this collection for their own studies, at times without acknowledging their source. We feel it is time to acknowledge the man who has borne the heat and burden of the day involved in making this collection. Of course, the ultimate origin of this collection is the Warlis themselves, and it is to them that we dedicate this monograph.

Rudolf C. Heredia

INTRODUCTION

"Once upon a time, there was a king who ruled over the kingdom of Jawhar. He was the ruler of the Warlis. His Kingdom was attacked by a neighbour, Popera, the Koli king. Popera demanded that he be given only that much of land that could be covered by a cattle hide. The Warli king agreed to this demand. Popera then covered the entire Warli land with a cattle hide. Thus the Warlis lost their kingdom." This loss is still today remembered by the Warlis and is symptomatic of their loss of identity today.

Indeed, the original affluent society (Sahlins 1963) finds itself at the cross-roads today. The Warlis find themselves in a situation where they have to take to agriculture for their subsistence, giving up on their earlier hunting-gathering habits, while the market forces stare them in their face.

We do not definitely know about the origins of the Warlis. According to a Sanskriti Kosa, the Warlis once inhabited the region near Dharampur, which has been described by Megasthenes as the Varalis. Many a scholars have argued that they derive their name from the region they once inhabited. Though it is a tempting line of argument to pursue, we today do not have sufficient evidence to independently corroborate this assertion. Interestingly, in the oral tradition of the Warlis, there is hardly any mention of the sea. The Warlis today need to be understood in the context of the present and against the backdrop of the forest laws that prove a watershed in the history of all gatherer-hunter communities.

The hunter-gatherers to a greater degree, and the pastoralists to a lesser degree have always been subjected to severe pressures by the agrarian communities. But in the precolonial era, such pressures were resisted, and sometimes reversed, especially in the Deccan. But the forests laws introduced by the colonial state have proved to be a major watershed in the history of these communities. The emergence of forests as major commercial entities in themselves altered the context and the colonial state asserted its right over the forest, which meant an active intervention in the day-to-day life of these communities, who depended for their livelihood on the forest. This direct control also meant an intervention in some of the traditional rights the people held over the forests. This fact introduced an altogether new system, where the traditional rights of wage-property obligations were replaced by the new ones (Gadgil and Guha 1992: 147)

Those changes affected different communities in different ways. The Chenchus for instance, were denied the right to hunt in the forest and were forced into a subordinate relationship with the cultivators. This in turn resulted in Chenchus being driven into banditry (Von Furer Haimandorf 1943). In another instance, the Baigas of central India lost their hunting skills, though their requirement for meat remained unchanged (Elwin 1959). In our case, the Warlis found themselves at the mercy of the money lenders, and found themselves at the door steps of a new subsistence system alien to their own. This exploitation and alienation resulted in the famous Warli revolt of 1940s.

Subsequent to the revolt, the condition of the Warlis remains by and large unchanged. They are still being denied the basic access to the forest, the rights of usage and the traditional duties and obligations that they once enjoyed over the forest. The fight for the forest has pushed the Warlis into a position where the very core of their culture is at stake.

It is this issue of culture which interests the compiler of this text. This work, we hope, shall be a small step in affirming the Warlis, their culture and their world view. There have been works on some other aspects of the Warlis prior to this one and we have learned a lot from them (Save 1943; Dalmia 1982). Save's is basically a classic old school imperialist ethnographer's account. His is naturally the first reference point on the ethnographer's map in charting Warli culture. His work is influenced decisively by the existing concerns of ethnography then and makes interesting reading today.

Dalmia's is a more recent study. Her concern is to interpret the Warli painting from within, i.e., from the standpoint of the Warli worldview. She has therefore delved into the symbolic and semantic nuances of Warli art. The legends, myths and the rituals of the Warlis have been interpreted accordingly.

Our concerns here are slightly at variance with the two works cited above. In this study we have primarily focused on the myths and the rituals, i.e., the mythos and the logos of the Warlis. Some of the rituals and myths are being documented for the first time through this work. The compiler has over a number of decades painstakingly collected these.

This work opens with the story of the "Wise men of the Warlis". Following on that are the creation myth and the stories of the corn goddess, Kansari. After these two are the life cycle rituals relating to birth, marriage and death followed by appendices. The flavour of the language as written by the compiler has been by and large preserved to do justice to his toil. It also provides the necessary authenticity to his work. The editor's responsibility was to carry out a research to verify the mythos as put together by the compiler, which hopefully has been adequately met. This work therefore is not a classical ethnographers account but is indeed a thick description in the ethnographic tradition. In the process of describing the mythos this work argues that the mythos is the logos for the Warlis!

AJAY DANDEKAR

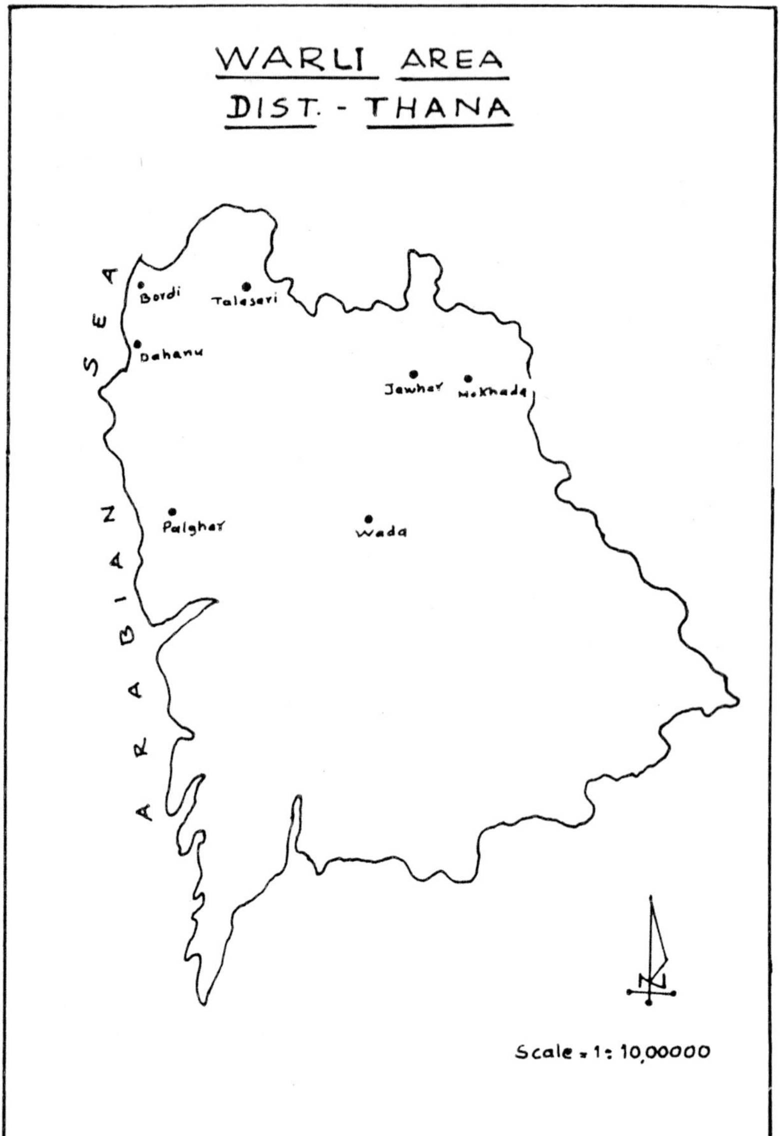
WARLI AREA
DIST. - THANA
ARABIAN SEA
Bordi
Talaseri
Dahanu
Jawhar
Mokhada
Palghar
Wada
N
Scale = 1: 10,00000

Contents

Chapter 1

THE BHAGAT : THE WISE MAN

Bhagats, the "wise-men" of the Warlis are the carriers and propagators of the Warli world view, which the community has acquired through its long existence in the forest. The knowledge of the medicinal plants in the terrain they live and the understanding of the different environmental parameters that regulate the Warli life are envisaged in their belief system. The Warli belief system thus is a manifestation of an intellectual attempt on the part of Warlis to understand the human behaviour and the nature. The rituals and beliefs of Warlis are adaptive to their living conditions. Thus, Warlis in a true sense are the "*juṅgalāce rājā*" (Kings of the forest) and Bhagats are the "wise-men" of the forest.

The belief system and the actual practice of rituals and rites exposes the dichotomy between the primitive thought and action. The Warli belief system has a strong pessimistic connotation which is expressed in terms of fear for evil spirits. As a contrast to it the propitiation and placation rituals and a strong belief in Bhagats give a clear indication of optimism vested in their ritual practices. So a critical understanding of the belief system and the rituals of the Warlis would not support a binary opposition between "self-fulfillment" and "self-abnegation" advocated by Yashodhara Dalmia (1982 : 35). Warli world view thus recognizes and falls in a "grey area" and it is the Bhagat who is responsible to maintain the equilibrium between the self-abnegation and self-fulfillment.

The pantheon of Warli gods suggests an animistic tradition as indicated by personification of several animals, plants and natural elements. The Warlis believe that all evils come from evil spirits. All sicknesses of persons, animals, crops and epidemics are caused by seven evil spirits : the vigna devis. Once upon a time god made seven beautiful ladies. ("The lived together for some time but soon began to envy each other and fought among themselves. They fought with their hands and their hands withered away. They fought with their legs and they became lame. They pulled each others hair and became bald.") Transliteration given below.

hātālā dharlia thiā loolia zālia
pāyālā dharlia thiā pāṅglia zālia
dokīalā dharlia thiā bodkyā zālia

One of the seven was an honest and obedient to god. She didn't like the sisters who fought bitterly with each other. She went to god and pleaded for his intervention and asked for justice. God, moved by the request punished the ladies. He sent one flying in the air who became *āsra* (*Apsarā*). He deported one to the earth and she became *dhartī*. Another he punished by sending her to the hills, thus she became the *savria baī*. The remaining four became unfortunate *vigña baiya* who are responsible for all ailments of the living beings.

The Warli intellect, thus holds different evil spirits responsible for some common ailments of human beings and personify them to call them by different names. *Ungavita baiya* causes small fox, *gavriya baiya* causes measles (*Govrī*), *vanjlia baiya* causes chicken pox (*Kasarda/kānjlī*), *tilibaiya* responsible for something like chicken pox, tani baiya brings large size small pox, *kaarndia bāiyā* facilitate the growth of big size lumps on the body which resembles karanjia seed. Thus most of the ailments are due to these evil women spirits.

The male Gods are often depicted as good spirits such as Yesu Gavlia. He is depicted as the saviour from all these ailments. Thus Yesu Gavlia is also known as Bahramba or Baharm and is manifested by a long broom with peacock feathers which is wrapped in a cloth and kept against the hut, well protected from dust and smoke. During Divali celebration it is taken from one house to another by either one of the elders or by a Bhagat. Though Yesu Gavlia is powerful over the evil spirits, most of the prayers and sacrifices are made only to evil spirits (vigna baiyas). It appears that all the evils that comes over the Warli society must be got rid off by placating the evil spirits, and for all the good that comes to the Warlis, comes from the good spirits. Thus Warlis believe both in placation and propitiation, but never mix them together. The placative rituals are carried out in utmost perfection and the occasion of propitiation is celebrated with pomp and solemnities. The good spirits are powerful in themselves but do not seem to have any jurisdiction over the evil spirits.

The Warli worldview, their value system, their organization, social and religious beliefs and cults are thus embedded in their belief in spirits. The good spirits are hidden and need not be disturbed. Thus, one sees the negative attitude to the good spirits. They placate the evil spirits and believe that the good spirits take care of themselves.

The religious and social rites are done out of fear. The popular belief among Warlis is that if the evil spirits are made happy, they themselves will be happy. These spirits are usually personified in a sick person, trees, fields, hills, animals, etc. The Bhagats are male and witches are female, hence every woman is a potential witch who are ill-treated by the Bhagats by accusing them of some evil in the village. There are *zun* Bhagats who have the capacity to be possessed by the evil spirits, narrate the cause of offense to the Bhagat and people around and demand sacrifices for placation. For example in the placation ceremony of vaghia deva (the boundary God), the Bhagat gets possessed and reveals the offenses committed by the party and asks for offerings. The Bhagat then promises the offering and asks the evil spirit to forgive and bless the farmers.

The Warlis believe that the evil spirit can take hold of the person and torture him with all kinds of maladies. The good spirit can enter into the Bhagat and suggest remedies, since he is also the medicine man, he can suggest some remedies with rituals and rites. The Bhagat is only a man of god, a "*bhakta*" of god and his knowledge of medicines is a gift of god. The Warlis have a strong faith in their Bhagat.

The Warlis are strong believers in the life after death. They are scared of the dead who go into the hands of devil to become evil spirits. They have the tendency to appease rather than to confront the situation by personal effort. All their failures in life are attributed to the power of the evil spirits and day by day the Warlis become helpless.

The Warli Bhagats are not born, they are made. A new Bhagat is trained by an old Bhagat from his childhood. The candidate is chosen before the age of puberty (about 12 or 13 years old). The parents pay for the training of their son. The candidates undergo a serious and rigid training period. Usually it begins sometime in May and ends with Divali. The whole training lasts for several years, with regular exams before the panchas of the village. The students have to abstain from all kinds of meat, such as also spicy foods and curries. He can only eat *chapātī* and rice with salt or some light chutney. He should avoid eating in noisy places, hence they prefer the foot hills or banks of the rivers.

If while eating he hears the sound of bangles, he should leave his meal and have it at a later time. While in training he should not converse with virgins. He keeps the secret about the type of lessons learned : the *Khands*, he is taught. There are several children who ask these students about the training, but are not easily disclosed. The candidates usually avoid grass cutting, tree cutting and take care not to harm any living creature.

During the monsoon, Bhagat takes students to the outskirts of the village, a little hut is made and the teaching starts there. The following *khandas* (chants) are taught to the students.

1. Mahadeva Khand (creation myth)
2. Palicha Khand (for injuries on bodies)
3. Baiyancha Khand (for women)
4. Mudhicha Khand (blowing on pain spots)
5. Kansari Khand (for crops).

These chants are taught daily word by word. The Bhagat chants the *pada* from these khandas and candidates follow him. Thus they memorize the Khandas word by word.

There are two other Khandas which are bit lengthy and have several minor khandas in them. They are *Dis* Khandas and *Jāat* Khandas. But these two Khandas are optional to the candidates but essential for the *dis*-Bhagat.

For all these, the candidates face a test which confirms them as a Bhagat. The elder members of the hamlet along with the Bhagat go to a lonely place in the forest. A spot is cleaned and cow dunged. A circle of *supāries* (beetle nuts) is made on the floor. The elders sit in a circle and the Bhagat asks the candidates to chant the Khandas. After the successful rendering of the Khandas and with the consent of the elders the candidate is declared as passed. The candidate then cuts the throat of a cock and thereby breaks his long abstination from the taboos imposed upon him during the training period.

After the candidate becomes free from the taboos, he appears in a second test. Four suparies along with a heap of flour are made on the ground which represents four khandas. The Bhagat and the elders decide which supari represents which khanda. This is kept secret from the candidate and he is asked to choose any two among the four and to name them. If he succeeds in that he is allowed to practise those two khandas. In case of a failure the candidate has to appear for the same test next year. The fresh Bhagats are allowed to practice only two khandas at the beginning. In the following years he may choose two more and so on down the years, as he gains experience. It takes several years to become a full fledged Bhagat.

The tradition of paying *guru dakshiṇā* continues with the Warlis. The candidates generally pay in cash to the teacher. A cock is then cooked, in the traditional way and consumed by those present. Drinks are also served to all members.

The vocation to Bhagat is becoming rare. The young educated children do not agree to undergo the training. The old Bhagats are of the opinion that there is no faith among the youngsters in the art of Bhagats and feel shy to perform the religious ceremonies. Many of them now call a local Brahmin and make their ceremonies short. Though the young generations do not trust the Bhagat, somehow they have deep seated fears about the spiritual powers of the Bhagats.

The Bare Foot Doctor

Warli life is not only robed in environmental calamities, but quite often due to lack of balanced or adequate diet they fall prey to several physical ailments. In the Warli worldview, as discussed earlier all these ailments are due to the spirits that need to be propitiated or placated. The "wise-man", who is the saviour of Warlis from all these, seems to have knowledge about some medicinal plants. The success of the Bhagat in propitiating and placating the evil spirits and thereby curing the ailments not only depends upon his spiritual powers, it more meaningfully depends upon his knowledge and availability of medicinal plants.

Even today, though some rudimentary medical facilities are available in Warli areas, the Bhagat is the only life saver. The patient is generally brought to the nearest primary health center only when the Bhagat so desires. It is a pity that the health service in the Warli land is so ephemeral that often the patient dies due to the absence of the medical officer or due to a lack of availability of the proper medicine. In such a situation Bhagats with their age old traditional knowledge make a sincere effort to save the life. He considers himself as the "*bhakta*" of the god and believes that without the blessing of the god his endeavors will not be successful. The blessing of the god comes from the timely service to the people. That is why when any chance to serve the people comes, the "wise-man" runs on bare foot to save the patients from an untimely death. Hence he is justly called a "bare foot doctor".

The "wise-man" doctor, helps the Warlis in their minor to major health problems. According to the Warli worldview the distinction of major and minor ailments depends upon the involvement of the evil spirits. So they believe that some of the evil spirits are more dangerous than others. Following this kind of a belief, propitiation and placation becomes the only way for the remedies. The minor ailments like simple wounds, fractures, etc., are treated more by administration of herbal medicine and the "wise-man's" spiritual power is less required in these matters. But in the major ailments the "wise-man" plays the central role. In case of any vigna the Bhagat is approached and consulted to identify the reason for the ailment. The Bhagat diagnose it in his own traditional method. The Bhagat then goes for a placative ritual to know which bhutālī is responsible for the vigna. The details of this ceremony is delineated in the following paragraphs.

Whenever a person is sick or there is an epidemic the evil spirit : *bhutālī* is believed to be responsible. Bhagat tries to identify the *bhutālī* who has caused the said ailment. This is known as *divā nāṅgne* or diagnosis. Bhagat takes a winnowing fan and lays the rice pundaliyas, three on the top line, three in the middle and three at the end. Four heaps are then put at the center. At the side a spherical shaped ring is made with rice.

bhoot pis dushman dagā ahe kaī bāt
devāci dagā ahe
taye bālkāci
bandobast karoon de
anna khātā pānī pitā karoon de
yo tuyīavar bhār ahē
cander surya cā kiran moklā
tar hya bālālā moklā jālā

pāhije : panc divsācī bayeni dharat hai (See app. 1.) (Tr. : Is there evil sprit, enemies ill-will or it is from god. Is it from child, if so help find it. Make the salty water drinkable. This is your responsibility. The ray of the moon and the sun and the stars are free.)

The Bhagat after the chanting of the *khandes* takes the grain of rice in a pinch of his fingers and keeps them by pairs...seven pairs...then he takes another pinch and goes on. If the pair happen to be the same then the sickness if from god, if not it is from the evil spirits.

If the sickness is from god, a figure is made from rice flour with fourteen "*shira*". This figure is left on the place with some sindoor on it. It is passed twice over the head of the sick person and then taken to be thrown into the river.

As the four pallets are being fixed on the figure the following words are said : vighnacā devā...pirmāli bhāg...dāvani bhāg...darungā bhāg...ālā śidā dara za...pach pavle moghare...

The second figure is dāyicā deva = carvasi mānus rupia. It is made to sit on the palasa leaves with some tumeric powder on it...passed on the head of the sick twice and taken to the river.

Fourteen rice heaps are laid on the floor in the following order.

X	X	X	X	X	X	X	X	X	X	X	X	X	X
1	2	3	4	5	6	7	8	9	10	11	12	13	14.

1. mahādeva...
2. soni jal...
3. rūpā jal...
4. pāvāsā deva...
5. vavdi vera...
6. cander surya...
7. kiran moklā
8. vighnā...
9. cārvasi devī
10. nirvaal deva...
11. dagdī deva...
12. sahal deva...
13. kurti deva...
14. vīra deva...

The Bhagat taking rice in hand passes from left to right saying Oh god the great healer...heal the sick.

After the diagnosis is over, the "wise-man" proceeds to the evil spirit. Different evil spirits need to be propitiated by different methods. The wise-man takes the help of different ritual patterns which are a calculated combiton of the application of herbal medicines and the chanting of specific *gāvlis* from different khandas. In the next chapter the details of different propition and placation rituals along with the khandas used in the occasion are discussed at length. Before we proceed to that let us know some of the common herbs that the wise-man uses in curing different health hazards. Following are the most valuable medicinal plants that are available in the Warli land to help the wise-man in curing the diseased Warlis :

1. Karvi—This plant is found in all the hills of the Western ghats. It flowers after twelve years or so. The roots of this plant are used widely by the Warlis for the treatment of jaundice. A table spoon of the root extract thrice daily is given to the patient. The results are very encouraging.

2. Deni—The stem and the roots are made into paste with the white of the egg and is applied to the fracture.

3. Dagadphodī—Leaf and root juice is taken for three weeks, daily three times for stone in the bladder or kidney.

4. Borada—Leaf juice is applied in simple injuries like cuts and wounds. It burns like iodine.

Apart from this, the wise-man plays a major role at the time of any kind of communal calamity : *vigna*. When a general calamity comes over a village, the wise-man is approached by the elders or those suffering from any common sickness. They take some rice and go to the Wāghobā deva and make the pūjā. Rice heaps are made in the name of the gods to be placated in front of the Wāghobā. The following prayer is said :

He devā hi vighnā āli
Tāpī vighna : āgī vighna
Adia dāvnā
Karjīa dāvnā
murdyā dāvnā
cāvtī dāvnā
hi vighna ālī ahā; āplyā gāvāt
gāvia deva tu pāthiśī ubhā rāhī jos;
kānā dāvaal aikoo; pan doli khal nāi nāngoo
tā tulā kharī mānū
khali yetī tā varoōn ghālav jos
vārīin yetī tā cāloon ghālav jos

āsā deva pāthiśi ubhā rahi jos
nārlacā fal jāmīn thevat āhā
sendarace dabbe; dhupāce parmal
asa gavat vigna ala nāi pāhije
te door kar jos; hi punja tula chadthi hoyil
cārhi khanda zāmin; donhi yuga jāmin
ātha kot rājā zāmin; nav kot khanda jāmin
ye khandace deva jāmin navsālā ubhā raha jos;
rande mundecā navas
porā bālaacā navas
dhor adharancā navas
tai setī vādicā navas; motha navas ahe
hya navasālā ubhā rahe jos
payae ade nāi alā pāhije; shire kade ala pahije
sitlāi devai gav sital thev jos
pānī praman sital; dooha praman nital thev jos
hivse samindar hivā pad jos
tathe samindar gavat tandha padjos. (See App. 1.2)

(Tr. : O god, these evil spirits have come, they are of fever and of other calamities. O god these evils have come to our village. O god of our village stand by with us, be here by our years, dream with our eyes and we believe in you. If evils come down to earth send them back before they land. Dispel them from the earth. O god stand by us, please be with us. We keep the coconut as a witness, we keep the lead powder and the smoke of incense for you. Such evils should not come to our village. Send them off. This puja is being offered to you. The four corners will stand witness, the two worlds will stand witness. O god of the world stand witness. This is the offering of the people, of the children of the cattle and of the fields and the gardens. Stand by the side of the newly born. Let him not come out with feet first, let him come out with head first. Goddess of purity, keep the village pure. Keep it clean like water, white like milk. Keep the wild sea cool, let it keep the village cool.)

After the ninth day the wise-man takes *kunkoo*, *gulāl* and *abīr* which is applied to the eye-lids...and counts each one of them on a plantain leaf spread in front of him. The counts are as follows...Āttā...(flour of rice)...is counted in small pinches...in thousands...from 1...2...3...till 20,000. *Kunkoo*...in small pinches...counted in hundreads from 1 to 20, gulāl...from one thousand till 17,1700, abīr from 1 to 14,1400. Then, taking the name of the spirit he gets possessed and the reaction begins. If the spirit, enters into him then that spirit is responsible for that sickness. Thus the diagnosis is correct and the patient is on the way to recovery. The plantain leaf is spread over the head and the body of the patient and is then thrown into a river or a pool of water outside the village. A coconut is broken and one piece is thrown in the river and the other is enjoyed by the wise-man.

One of the greatest threat to the Warli life is their vulnerability against the hazard of snake bites. This is only to be expected, since the Warlis live in huts and around thick forests. During the monsoons, when the fields in the low lying areas are flooded, the snakes crawl up to the high lands. It is the time when the frogs and rats are in plenty and make a good meal for the snakes. The huts are dark and stored with fire-wood, seeds, etc., and the snakes find a corner for themselves. They often hide in small pots, baskets, rags, etc. During the night the Warli goes without light. He follows the trodden path, where the snakes coil themselves for warmth. During summer the path is cooler due to the beaten dust. Most of the snake bites are reported during the grass cutting season, where hundreds of Warlis migrate to the distant grass lands for a meagre sum of money to repay the loans they have taken during the months of starvation. Often women, who collect fire-wood to make a living, suffer fatal snake bites.

In several villages the Bhagat is the only life saver. Only when the Bhagat fails, the case is brought to the nearest medical officer who at times is absent and may not have the necessary medicines and means. Very often it is too late and the person is left to die.

As soon as the wise-man is informed about the snake bite he makes haste and carries with him the required herbs. The patient is examined by him and from the symptoms he knows the type of the snake that has bitten the patient. He administers the first dose of the herbs and begins his chants. He sits near the patient with a bunch of leaves from the Abeta tree (leaves used by the warlis to make Bidi). He keeps striking the patient on the injury while Chanting the following :

sakālcia paharī suryāta ugavlā āhe
yānī ta kirnā sodilī ahā
molata samdiria kirinita ujedla
cārī ti khaṅdāta kirinitā ujedley
gayīcī ti bhīrdhi ta sutlī ahā
ahā ti tānā padā gāyīcī ti
cūrāyālā lagli ahai
varlī ti kumda ti tāceti carāyālā lāagli āhai
tasanch te nighoon te gela ahai
tasānc te sidhace budāsī gela to
vansīce jādāvar ujvā hāt tākalā āhai
pālā tho todalā āhai, colato malāto
ras kadhalā āhai, tasatā surpantane
mirithā māngīnī surpanthe dusla āhai. (See App. 1.3)

(Tr. : The sun rises early in the morning and sends its rays to the four corners. The calfs let lose and they go for grazing. They graze on the slopes and go towards the date trees, they hold on to the herbal plants and remove the leaves, smash the leaves on the hand and rubbed where the snake has bitten.)

While still fanning the patient the Bhagat continues the chant while the helpers administer the herbs.

nāthaguru ādhamnāg—sukha sodoo-sodavikhā
pāsana ballōo—yere vikha—kotho hotās—daslās to
tujī vikhā—tuji laharā siplī kāṭhī, paila fool
gānīvānī, vidyā ghetlā harāvantī, ye re vikha
kothē āhaai—sutītī, vālalā āhai.
are sāpā hōtas kotha—tujhēe kāncī
maru arap devroo, sardīce taicī ta kāncī hotta,
taaita arapdevroo, phorsācyā kāncī hotta, arap devroo.
āre vikhā vala āhe,
tuje vikhā, tujī lāhare pānia sārkhā

thevalī naha, dudhāsārkhī sital zālī, nital zālī.
miriyā mir gur khi, tāmbolkī, sisaarkī, pāharabadu,gopī
bhagat mere sāngāyā ya gāyā kasia duslia,
jānvere nīgore...vigore... (See app 1.4)

(Tr. : O leaders of the Nath gurus...the first snake you have left the poison, come where are you, you have left your poison. Where are you, o serpent, I wish to remove the poison. O poisonous one, your venom is like water, clean as water, white as milk.)

The first dose is of the extract of the leaves from Anon (sitaphal) of about half the cup. The second dose is from the extract of the Kardode leaves of about half a cup. The third dose is the extract from the bark of the Gorda tree : half a cup. The fourth dose is the extract from Tenda leaves (Warlis call it Lal deth—a tall purple plant with flowers and tiny seeds). The fifth dose is from the Sag tender leaves (sagpan deth). This extract is passed through a white cloth and the drops are put in the nose of the patient. The above crushed leaves are put on the wound. These doses are administered at an interval of few minutes and after the last dose is administered the bhagat or the patient inserts his finger into the throat to provoke vomiting. As soon as the patient vomits the bhagat examines the vomit by lifting it with a stick. If the sticky stuff hangs on the stick, the doses are then repeated twice or thrice till the sticky matter is no more. Then some salt or chilly is given to feel the taste. Once the taste is normal then it is considered that the poison is out and the patient has a hope of survival. Immediately, after this the juice of chamli bark is administered. Another dose of the pal tree bark is given and the patient is told to be quiet and calm and is asked to rest. If the snake is a phorsa (viper), an additional dose from the extract of karyil root is given to induce vomiting. If it is a krait (which the Bhagats say is very fatal) a dose from the extract of Banana tree roots is given to the patient to induce vomiting. These doses are given before the chamli and pal since they are meant for vomiting poison. It appears from the above that the Bhagats preoccupation is to induce vomiting at any cost. The above medicines are given for all kinds of poisoning. Several cases of snake-bites have been cured by these herbs, provided they are administered in due time.

The gāvlis or the chants uttered by the Bhagats and the invocations are a spiritual means to detect the type of poison. They also help the patient to keep his calm and trust in the divine powers that affect the cure. The Bhagat keeps a watch over the patient till he is out of danger.

The Bhagat feels happy when the patient improves. He normally does not ask for any fees but will accept *dakshina* if given by the patients household. Several Bhagats give several herbs to induce vomiting but we have chosen a reliable and widely used method. The Bhagats feel that sometimes the herbs do not work in cases where the patient is heavily drunk or has exerted himself too much by running from the place of snake-bite which is often done and proves to be fatal. Sometimes a delay in finding the herbs soon specially in the nights proves fatal for the patient. These extracts from herbs cannot be stored since they seem to lose their efficacy. The Bhagats were happy when told that a Snake Bite Kit is available from the Haffakine Institute. But the exorbitant cost is beyond the reach of poor Warlis.

The Bhagat thus emerges as the fulcrum around which the entire belief system of the Warlis revolves. He is thus the sole custodian and mediator between them and the god. Also he is looked upon by the Warlis as giver of life, a medicine man par excellence, whose knowledge of saving life is derrived from divinity.

Chapter 2

MAHADEV KHAND : THE CREATION MYTH

This is the first Khand taught to the candidate. It is the chant to the great God, the Mahadeva. It consists of many sub-sections.

Sakālcā pāhār to lāglaa āhe; candar; surya;
cāndya yānā kiranā sodali āhe
samindar ujeḍat tasā to kāyāl
mahāmati mahādeva varata; gaṅgā; gouri
ukhalat; musalat; khāvarang;
ghetali āhā; sonī te maalvari cadhalī āhā
koryā padlyā āhā.
khādyālā saḍakā tāndul kele āhā
tase ti andherī kholīlā gelī āhā; kangāl to topā tasi
cholali dhovlī; dhānlī
agnebal lāvlā āhā; panī tāvlā vajrā
silā pāni nelā āhā; thevlā āhā
mahādevā hākā mārli āhā; āngholi karāayā lāglā āhā
dātvani ghetli āhā; jivaicā chānfal
dharativar tāklī āhā; tyācyā gandoolāta jamalā
lohate mārgilā calalā, candar
surya kiranāt sodalī āhā,
gandoolicyā marnā zālī.
tasā gāndoolyā dharticyā pāthīt gelā āhā
dharaticā karnār zālā āhā
bhātāt gangāta gourī hï tayār kelī āhā
mahādevā hākā mārlī āhā
jevanālā jivnā hāt dhuvale āhā
gural tasā to uthlā āhā
moyaticya kādyä ghetle āhā

sonācyā jal ghetle āhā
barāt benti tatha devālā hākā mārli āhā
tasā mahādevān bolavalā
devācyā pārodī beslī āhā
tasā zālā tar phodun dilā
bhātāce viganāce jal;
girmulāce cal phodun tū dijās
tasī tī vighna dharun bāṅdhun dilā
rakhawālece merī kāthī (māṅjī)
jihīr hunā tāp kādhun
ghijā divsāṅ vārā.
candar surya jagatā
cānd jagtāt zālā āhē
sukesar jagat zālā āhē
jagesvar jagat zālā āhā; vijesar jagat zālā āhē
gadhesar jagtā; jagtāṅ zālā āhā;
māzā zālā to (kansaricā jal) phodun dilā
(dushman sharum de)
khairesar jagatā; bhoyesar jagatā,
yā jāndeva jagat gaurī jan deva jagat;
nakesar deva jagata zālā āhā;
taseca vighṅā dharun bāṅdhun dilā;
bālā dharativar padlā āhā
dharun bāṅdhun deva ho dijā
ātā kaje dāve te hātāce bhānsī
gurucā mān, phulālā bhār āla āhā,
candar suryācā kiran to moklā karjo;
tasā bālā hïṅdtā karjo;
unhā to tāp to kādhun ghijā de;
vāvdhī vārā varset;
rājhālā ramat, baram deva varce rājāla āhē
mādheri deva to
tatha humāya deva varce rājāla devāt kelā āhā;
halket jagatāt kelā āhā;
mothe samīṅdar olāde jagta
hī sen gorānbiyā saṅdīratā him basāyā

hisan samdīr tasā jagtā kelā āhā
tadahet samdīr sitlyā samdīr
sital stalya samdīr
sital nital karun samīdaro
hātobā deva sāvrān karīt āhā
patsed cār pathūn pāca ūbhā rahajā
sapārce velīt karjā; rajīt povetlā sātse upte rahajā
veghāṭē nadgāsī zobīt nāko sāvjā
vaghacā dhoṅīt karjā
gurucyā pāṭhisī ūbhā rahajā
jivdāni (devi) jagti mahādevāca dovlā japtā
tasā vvaticā chedā jagata
makrit chedā jagtā zālā āhā
hubāce zād jagtā
tiparibā deva jagtā zālā āhā
sunāt māndav jagtā zālā āhā
sonicā darvājā siva, jagtā zālā āhā
mahā laksmi jagtī zālī āhā
vajrābāi tulsābāi jagtāt
kalkādevi jagtyāt
vighnā dharun bāndhun dijā
ambai jagtyāt
nimaydevī sitlaydevi jagtyāt
māzā nitlay deva rāntaydevi jagtyāt
masāydevi jagtyat zālyā āhā;
tasā to gāvchā deva jagtā
āpalyā gāvālā vidanā āli āhā,
dharun bandhun dijā
gurucā mān karāt
gāy gavlī padhli āhā
kuthnī hīntin hānavās gāyīce
cārāyālā lāvjās jagli chedā mahārt jagat.
devā ho karat āhā māzā jal, bhūtāce vighnā
nāvācā zālā koret ghātāt āhā,
phodun dijā go dhānolelā chedā jagtā zālā āhā
gārdi chedā zālā āhā,

Mutt
sakāl pāharā lāglā āhā;
tasā candar to suryā ugun te ālā āhā;
kirnā sodli āhā;
mul samidar kirnā ujedlā;
tasī gaṅgā gauri nighūn geli;
tasi sāvrang supāt ghetli āhā,
sonīt mālāvarati chadli āhā;
tasi kansare pādli āhā
khādānā katli āhā
kanī konadā vāyalā kela āhā;
pahalā gaṅgā gauricā nivādā lāglā;
ātā khālche rājelā mīrikat (manus) tasā;
rām laxman rām deva;
are pan dādā tulā kāy zālā āhā;
māze doke cāvar potāt aag; zāli āhā;
āra pan dādā nā bhūto (bhiu nakos)
khānagācā dongrālā jāt āhā,
hudūn hule; kādhale
deva hiṅdāyā lāglā āhā;
hotī tānhelā; potīt dukhelā
malā fār tahān lāgli āhā,
malā kāy ātā karāvā,
pāus nāy pānī nāy mīla,
todlyāt hātī khargā (koytī) ghetlī āhā
tasā gaṅgā rāgāt nighūn galāce budāsi gelā,
phātkā gāl (kātevālā zād) todūn padlā āhā,
khālpat dharatīce thocā mārlā āhā,
dharati toḍūn vansāyā kadhlyā āhā; mooth udkālā dhāvā toḍlyā āhā
rāmā yen ubhā rahalā āhā;
don pāthar ānalā āhā;
vanseyā kuthle āhā;
tasyā colalyā nāyi rām nāy vighanā;
nighā ātā kāy karāvā?
tari pan dādā nako bhījo

phirun battis usil (dongar) canecā zādāsī gelā āhā
ubhā rahālā āhā;
canecā budāvar cadhāya lāglā āhā;
unvat nādrat marat āhā;
nāy pāni pāus mil tasā
devānī khand tasā nādālā marat nāhī,
pāni pāus milat
laksīman deva kasā khasā disi zālā āhā
mangā rākh nādrāt tarī pān pāni
pāus nāy to mil
tasyā māvaltasī nādārat mārlya canyāce;
zādāvarsī nilā bāl sangatī
ticyā sārovar pāni nānglā āhā;
canyāce dhartīvar devlā āhā;
muth adklyā gāvāt sodylā āhā
sarovari jān ubhā rahalā āhā;
muthi adaklyā kalaṅgadī nid kelyā āhā
pānīt budāvāyā nelī āhā,
balatin sāvarīce hākā mārle āhā
dādā nako pānyālā hāt lāvjos māzā pāni de;
hiravā gār thanḍ āhā
budāsi gelā āhā;
ujīt pān todle āhā;
kolhā vālā āhā;
pāni ghetlā āhā;
muthi odokalyā dāvā de bārā belotni āle āhā;
vātecā khanḍā cur bhukhā zālā āhā,
nighun cālalāy kelice khaṅhāsī kelī;
phirun padli āhā;
tasi mirīk mājācī dukhā muthīce
cāvalāce bhārākhāl muthī valūn te dijāt
tasā rāmā laksimann deva ālā āhā;
rāmāce jāyālā zāle āhā;
vanasāyā khuḍla aha
colalyā ras vanasāyācā kādhlā āhā;
rāmālā eesvar devācii nā baramadeva mivadā de;

satī jivdā satyecā lihīn
tagdīr kharī līhel havā
muthice khandekhāl tasī guruce shabdākhāl utarat;
khāli nāy utarsī cāvalī suryācā kiran
mokalā āhā
tasyā tyā muthī lāgun gelyā āhā;
tasā bārālā chāvrā (cāyti) sodlā āhā;
āag zālī āhā;
guruce devjī gurā bhimā gurā;
dhali guracā muth vālun dijo,
guruce sabdākhāl nāy vālsi tulā priyā tasā
malā nāhi priyā lāglā;
cāvryā muthī; ālyā muthī tākalyā muthi cālvas muth
yā muthī guruce shabdākhāl nikāl; gurubābā
tyā jātē; tānpar jāte van jalte; gurubābā tapān kar;
bodhanā kar; tasyā muthi vālun desil nāy
vālasī māze guru ghālasī magāre valsī
ḍāve te pāyāci lāth mārun tasī muṭh vālun deu;
ābhālat cānd basalā āhā;
dharatilā pathār basālā āhā;
tasā bālāca bān basalā
samdhī nirmal zālā āhā;
palkhākhand garajāy gaṅgā gauri nighūn geli āhā;
kāy karāva tāpale gāyice sināt
topli āli āhā
sakālce pāharālā uthle āhā;
tasī kasārā mānīlā sinā gavasāyā lāgli āhā;
tasī bāruth mānīlā geli āhā;
tasī sināt nāy milat āhā,
Pālkhi Khand
pāthisī ubhā rahajās rātila sāt pheryā
dukhāsi ubhā rah
jintit bāi (manus) ticvā kārnī nighun
ātā kuhalā bāl gāyice potāsī nighālā
chānglyā tyā cjāmbḍā konāyā lāglā āhā;
cāndar yekdā deva pāthsīlā ubhā

karnibāi barnibāi tōṭlibāi midlibāi randecā dukhācā
sad band kihun jāti ho
vanse konāche nāvi marat āhā
dukhāce nāvi tasī nighun cālalayā
dhartīcyā khoharnyā zalyā āhā;
tasyā tyā dukhācyā koharyā karat āhā;
gurāce shabdākhāl devāce nāva mothī karam khotā
karāl are pun devānī akkal nāglā hotā;
tasā āj te cālāyā lāgolā āhā;
hatī kāhi dijās majece pramesar devāce pāya
hāt dole tond bolāyā cālāyā didhil āhā;
tasā hindatā karun tasī dukhā mārūn
geli āhā;
tasi soharatī cālāyā lāglī āhā
cānd suryācyā kohornyā zalī āhā;
mi tyācyāt nāhi mīrkīt
māyzāce dukhāce kohorne (kam karane) karīt āhā,
tasā sukesar deva tyācyā kohornyā
tasi nighun te tharasān dukhāt zijat nāy;
komabat nāy bhukat phitat nāy
yelā kāy karāva
nighun lāglā āhā;
mahādeva gangā gauri cālaye lāglī āhā;
varāt beloti geli (doghā) getī āhā;
tasā sonyācyā dāri devālā hākā mārālyā āhā;
deva jamā zāle āhā (lāglā āhā)
devā tū bājulā basajos to bājūlā basalā;
pavsyā deva bolāyā lāglā āhā;
tasā yu mālāt jātice bāher basavalā āhā;
kuhalyā gāyi dhavas
tasā yo jātice kāy re pun malā jātiche bāher basavalā
magā devācā tumhālā ātā rāgāce
devākada jāyālā lāglā āhā,
rohanīcā pāni padāyālā lāgalā āhā;
tasī biyā ugūna alī āhā;
tasā dudhicā tānā (vel) phutlā āhā;

cār medīcyā lohāre gangā garjaye gelī āhā;
kurhād koitī karvane nighun gelī āhā;
geli gadh malālā sānace pāharālā;
teni jevanā keli āhā;
jivalī bhājlā nijlī guthlī āhā;
sakālce pāharāla khānagarācā dongarāla
velūt vāse todāyā lāgalā āhā;
dānḍe bāndhālā āhā ucalalā dokivar ghetalā āhā;
cālāye lāglī āhā;
māḍit māhalā ālī āhā;
sānace pāharālā mānḍav kelā āhā
tasā dudhi mānḍavāvar cadhalā āhā;
phulūn asā galful nirfal
yekuch dhudhī lagalā āhā;
tasā dhudhi vādhalā āhā
pikāyā jog zālā āhā
dhudhīcī poṭāt palēce khanḍ nighālā
karane bharane rānde tasī kelī āhā;
sahaj poṭat majīce poṭit pahalī ji aag
zali āhā;
tasī dukhā vadhāyā dāne pahal (payal) lāgli āhā
ātā vicār gharisi aai bāp karāyalā
hī kāy dukhā zālī āhā;
karaniyāce kārani chālalī āhā;
ti bī tasā palecā khand
cālāyā tumacē devācī karani biyā varunī biyā
kohoraniyā mazyāji pahātce devā kutalbālā
māzyācā karatec bharanecā kohun tākajāt
devācā pāy didhel na
tasā nābhūtā (bhiu nako) nākos
bihajos pālecā khand cālat āhā;
tasi hātācī pāhāncī dukhā karani biyā bharani biyā
todli biyā modli biyā; āj pāhatesi
uthūn jāyajos
har mojālā deva āhās
garajācā kuhalebālā

sahaji pāhanice shabdākhāl
tākat vanagān vahat āhā;
tākatici āmi jevanā rāndhūn de;
dādā deva bolāvā lāglā āhā
samīdar kadīt kāpat jat basalā āhā;
samīdar hūn samidar sosun samdīr ghātalā āhā;
gāy bārā varsā zālī āhā;
jāgelāch gāyicā tanḍ khapūn deva
tāgaḍe lolāyā lāglā āhā; marun jat lāglā āhā;
tevadhvāt yichārāt tasī dukhā manjyāce pāhānace
rujun phiṭūn ni sukhavāni khaṇda
rohaḍe mānilā geli āhā;
gāyicā shenāt gavasāyā lāgli āhā
hivāle mānilā geli āhā;
tasī shena nāy milat āhā
murum mātīlā geli āhā;
tarī pan shena nāy milat
magā tambaḍ mālālā geli āhā
gāyicī shenā milālī āhā
tasī bahanacī pātī bharlī āhā;
hātāce jorākhālā māthvāvar madi māhalit āli āhā;
sanacī pāharālā rohanīcā pānī padāyalī lāgalā āhā;
todlyā sāt khānit khanalā āhā
teth sin tayār thevlyā āhā
teth sin tayār thevlyā āhā;
khāngar dongarālā geli āhā;
virkhanacā pālā ghetlā āhā
māḍi māhalela āle āhā
sakālce pāharālā uṭhali āhā;
lāgun sāt khanḍā dilā āhā;
rohinicā pāni padāyā lāgalā āhā
ata mālā yet pajalā āhā;
tasīch tulā te māhādeva bolāyā lāgalā āhā
tulā tyāci kaḍvyā karelāci biyā pāyjet āhā;
āmacyākade biyā karelācyā biyā nāhi milat
maga nighūn geli āhā;

pāthrīn rajyālā geli biyā magāyā lāgli āhā;
tikātīcyā biyā kaḍave dudhicī biyā
pāthri (udāri) bolāye lāgli āhā;
āmacekaḍe dudhyāci biyā nāhi āhā tasī
gugerī rājyālā gajarāya geli āhā;
tasī gungeri āmacekaḍa ghosālacyā biyā nāhi āhā
tasī bāy kulabyāce dārāsi garaj gauri geli āhā;
tumālā kām pāhāt
malā vayichā biyā sāt biyā ghetlyā āhā
sāt khanila lāvalī āhā (See app. 2.1)

(Summary Tr. : In the early hours of the morning the sun begins to dawn and flashes its rays across the earth, the sea shines, the earth smiles. The heaven proclaims the new day. The women Gaṅgā govrī lay their hands on the pounding rods and sit beside the threshing floor which they have just removed from their lofts with the help of small ladders for the paddy grains. They are busy polishing the grains, and white rice is ready. They then go to the dark rooms and scrub the untidy vessels, and wash them. The fire is lit, the water is boiled and carried to the threshold stone and the god is invited for a bath. He takes with him his tooth brush, tickles his throat and cleans his tongue, and bathes. He spits on the ground and the earth worm is born and it creeps along its own path, while the sun rays fall upon it and it struggles for life. The worm bores its way to the earth and feeds on the dust.

O great god Mahadeva, you have made the fields that yield and you invite me to eat. I have washed my hands and my face brushed my teeth with the twigs and gargled my mouth with the golden waters from the stream and invoked thy name. Come Lord and assemble thy kingdom, the Gods and Goddesses. Watch the streams of evils and calamities on this earth, control all fears, and the evil spirits, bind them and give them to me in bondage.

Give thy servant O Lord powers over the evil ones, the possessed poisonous waters and drinks, the heat and the fevers of all kinds.

Look O lord at thy heavens, the sun and the moon that scorch the earth worms, watch the sun God has awaken, hear the thundering Lord, the lightening sparkles, as the clouds burp each other, heavy showers follow and the fields overflow and floods, fill the earth. All your Gods and Goddesses, watch (Khaireshwar, Bhoheswar, Jana deva, Govari devi) the planets and all ask them O Lord to keep the evils in bondage.

Your child disciple on this earth asks for protection, give me the powers to bind all evils. There are blossoms in the fields. Let the rays of the sun shine propitiously on them. Let thy disciple roam around to cure fevers and those sick within it. Let all the Gods of thunder, clouds and rains be subject to Bahron, cast the evils of nature (Humai) into the sea, for they are defied.

The limbless O God invoke thee, the haves and the have-nots beg of thee. Stay by us in the bushes and tangles of life, watch our huts, protect us from the encounters with tigers and keep away from us their dens.

Assist our *gurus* (Bhagats) while they placate the sacrificial gods. The gods of our temples and villages, the protectors guard us from the Humba, the pipal and the tall trees, watch the boundaries of our village and the treasures of our mother earth. O Goddesses (Mahalaxmi Vairabai, Kalka, Ambabai, Tilasabai, Sitlabai, Nitlabai, Nasia bai etc...) intercede for us and be with us, as the Lord of our village watches our calamities. Respect O lord our *guru* (Bhagat) that he may teach me thy disciple the chants of the Govri (cows) that are grazed by the cowboys and sit under the protection of the village deities (chaddas) purify me and let virtue overflow to the limits of my village, where the spirits live.'

Several myths in the Warlis are very confusing and at times illogical. The Hirva Garbha is one of them. It mentions the Creation of living beings by God Hirva on this earth, through a certain woman Girjia (Girgi), a common name amongst the Warli women. There is the mention of Ihu which is interpreted by some Bhagats as a sister of Kansari. There seems to be a connection between Kansari myth and the Hirva myth. There seems to be a connection between Kansari (the grain) and Ihu the mother earth (Dhartari). Both need each other for their existence. The God Hirva is worshipped in many Warli Kul (Family Clan), is kept in the salad (basket) and puja is made in the house by the Bhagat.

There is relation of Girija during her pregnancy to trees like palas and some leaves that have red juice. Some mention is made of a pregnant cow, a hen, fishes in the river, the earthen pot...etc...it implies that all the living creatures...were made by the God Hirva. The word Hirva suggests greenery...living beings... Thus the baby born to Girija in the myth is Manjia a human being.

Chapter 3

KANSARĪ : THE LAME GODDESS

For centuries now the Warlis have remained aloof from other communities and their pantheon of gods and goddess. They have their own unique religious ceremonies and rituals and remain away from the mainstream religious movements though there is a cognizable attempt to sanskritise some of their (sentence not complete) cuttural practies.

Very little is known about the Warli origin and history. One of the ways to know some thing more about them is their rites and rituals which give some insight into their past.

The migration of the Warlis seem to be from the north. They do not sleep in the north-south direction. When they die they are laid facing the north, indicating the north as their ancestral habitat.

In some of the Warli rituals the Warli priestess has an important role to play, for instance, in marriage ceremony. *Dhavlerī* (priestess) performs the rite and one of the songs by the wedding lamp mentions the coming of the holy man from the north to witness the marriage. The *jolī* ceremony too is done by the priestess (Savāsinī). It is the ceremony of the initiation of the child into the Warli community.

The Warli creation myth about the universe mentions that the Mahadeva and the Gaurī are responsible for the creation of the Universe. It is a joint effort, the male and female partnership in creation. There is a mention of Mahādeva and Gaurī in search of seeds to fill the earth and the creation of *mānijā*, i.e., man. They go in search of the seeds to various places and contact farmers, there's a reference to the "Guṅgerī" (wasp). The Warli creation myth does not mention the traditional liṅga and yonī matrix.

In the Dhartari khand there is the mention of the Bull ploughing the mother earth. The Bull is a symbol of fertility and is used to explain creation in Warli myth. The Warlis even today have a religious ceremony called *rāas*, where the black goddess Kansari is honored and placated with the offering of the first fruits and grains of the new harvest. This once again implies the existence their worship of the goddess Kansari ("black Goddess")

Kansari Khand/(Wadicha Khand)
sakālce pāharīn tasi ti kulbin
nighun pārshācā dārām
Geli āhā ara dādā tū āmhā lā
jābudīcā holā nāgāyā geli āhā
māgun nāveṭā (bandhobast nāhi) disat
kumbudnici sheti pasant karāyā lāglā āhā
doghā kulbi vichār karat āhā
pāhun holyā pasant zālī āhā
māri tyā māhalālā geli;
sānace pāharālā jevan doghā kulbeche jevanā āhā
jevūn vichār karat āhā tase
āpunlā kāy pāyaje havā
sāt shet kamāri kulabīn lāglā āhā sanjān
shaharālā pārsī dādā
ikaḍa kamāri nāy milat āhā
tasīch boradi shaharālā kulabi vāḍolyāce dāri geli āhā
vichārāyā lāglā dādā kotha jāyacā?
malā kamāri sātashet shetō posāyā pāyajet
ikada kamāri hotī tī dhānā lāvāyā kelī lāvāyā
nighun gelī āhā : nāhishi kumāri milat
tasā kulabi cālāyā lāglā āhā
nighun pālghar saarālā gelā āhā
Tatha kamāri vānice dārasī
ikaḍa kamāri hotī pan sotāce kārkhānī lāvalī āhā;
nāhisi kamāri milat kulabī kasāvisā zālā āhā
māghāri valalā āhā cālāyā lāglā āhā
janmāt rājā gelā āhā
pāngar āicā janma zālā āhā
upjet upiyo rājā gelā āhā

dāsāca upjat zālā āhā
tvarit kamāri nāhī milat ruyī gāvāt gelā āhā;
ruyāt pujun te āli āhā;
tasyā kunbyāce wadīt, phulun mā tasī Pālset gāvī gurā cārāyā
gelī āhā. Tatha kamārī nāya milat sī, gāvace gurā cāri getī āhā.
sri gāvāt to gelā āhā
sirī jasī phulun ta bārā vāḍyā kunbyācyā yojo
atha taeāri gāvālā gelā āhā
sātse kāmāri tayārli
tasi toprilā bhiraḍ bharāyhā lāgalā āhā
sakālcā pāharālā ḍokīvar birād getli āhā
nighun lokā (mārgālā) chālāyā varce
rājāsi devāyā lāglī āhā
vāvaḍi varache hālpeḍ samdir ḍevaya lāgle āhā
javāri srāl hotī tāneri potī ti bhukelī
tasā te lahāni miṭāla mothe miṭāla
talapāti saharālā sātse kamāri ḍevāyā lāglī āhā
peti saharālā lahāni phāsyālā yeun
saharālā sātse kamāri
kulāmbi muharāpār chālat
tasī perotī saharālā tethun
lohāret mārgālā Chorgoan shaharālā āle āhā.
tasī Kojbaḍ saharālā āle āhā.
Manor gavāt kunbyāce dārāsi bhirāḍa ḍevārni
kamārila tasī basāyā sāngalā āhā
tasā āmalīt jevanā sātse kamārila tayār keli āhā
jevāli bolalī (sāvkās) āhā;
athā yi sāncece pāharālā nijali guṭlī
tasā yo kunbi sakalce bolāyā lāglā āhā;
koyati kurhāḍā mālā rokaḍā dām de;
lohārce dārī gelā āhā; Lōhār Koyata Kurādā Pājaun dijos; tyace
kama rajōt āhā
vālī athā vārathi dongarālā geli āhā hindāyā lāgli āhā
varālā nāy pasant sāngācā sāgvan
uglun geli āhā;
koḍyā koḍvāli ugḍun gelī āhā;

ināchā inavāli uglun gelā āhā
musal durgālā geli āhā vāral nāy mānat yei,
hinḍavale durngālā vāralā chitāmani nāy
ye tasī moharle durgālā geli āhā
nāy vāral nāgāyā lāglā āhā
koḍichā koḍāval bhārīl āhā
pār varāl ugasechi zāḍā bhārel
sāngāchā zādā vaḍālā bhārel āhā
māli māhālālā chālāyā tatha konāchā kon hotā
tina hākā dilā āhā;
tasī loṭice (sādhu) dārāsī naralāce
phalā dijos shidrāche dijos
tikeci bāṅgadicī punjā det māḍīt māhālālā ālī
kunbyācyā andher kholilā geli āhā
sātse kamārila bolāvā lāgli āhā
pandharā disācā sindāvārā karjos
vāral (jangal) toḍāyā jāyacā
rashi ḍongarālā geli āhā;
tatha devāchi vāvadit vāryāci; savareci
durgāci puja keli āhā;
shidrāchi nāralachi punjā kelī āhā;
vārli kombdici pujā kelī āhā;
varāl toḍāyā lāgli āhā
yek dis toḍāyā don dis toḍāyā;
tin dis; chār dis; pānch dis
pandhāra dis pan toḍun varāl purī kelī
nighun loti mārgālā ḍevāyā lāgli āhā
māḍit māhalālā āhā
sānce pāharālā nijāyā lāgli āhā
sakālace chandar-suryā kiranā soḍalī āhā
satset kamārilā hākā maralyā āhā;
nighun ālyā āhā;
tasi pāryā pāwatī ghetalī āhā;
jāmboticyā dolālā geli āhā
olāt bāndhāyā lāgli āhā
nāgvyā olhā disat hotyā sajavale āhā, phār bhāriyā;
āthā tasī kulboḍe olhālā bandh bāndi
karāyā lāgle āhā;
sānceci pāharālā jeṭhācā mahanā ungavalā

rohaīcā ugvatsī dhagdeva dhagāt
gājesar gajrāyā lāglā āhā
tasā yo kunbi nighun ungvatsi nadar tāk
satse kamārila hākā chalā ho kamāre ho,
vavrāt bharāyā jāv
nāral bharāyā lāgli āhā,
sāt phātā sāt rāv bharāyā lāgli āhā.
bharun rikāmi paḍli āhā,
vizeḍi māzyā tyā pāḍlyā āhā,
tasā rāph bharāyā lāglyā āhā,
tasā rāb aag lāglā āhā.
rāb peravlā
rohanicā pānī paḍāyā lāglā āhā,
soneti mālāvaṭi; phulavaṭi (gharvāli) chaḍjos;
biyā harekudāci javārici, chāvlici turici, āmbāḍicī,
nāglici
vālechī biyā, nāhisī milat
parsice biyā māngāyā geli āhā,
nāy biyā milat, māngat paṭāri rājālā geli āhā
pātari biyālā bolāye geli āhā, āmche kaḍa biyā nāy milat,
āmhāpāy patrācī biyā, tumce nāhi kāmāce
gunceri rajālā nāyse biyā milat,
mugal rājālā geli āhā,
nāy biyā vicārāyā tumhālā tyācāsī biyā pāyjet
hoti; āmhāpāy biyā āhāt;
vāniyāche dāri jāyjāte, korā rumāl ān jā
manga nāgliche biyā bheṭli āhā;
varicyā haricyā dāngicyā kuḍācyā
kolbyācyā getlyā āhā. nigun cālāyā lāgli āhā.
biyā māḍi māhalā chhin geli āhā;
gāicā gorha; virkhāce (sāgāce) buḍālā bāndhlā āhā;
nākāni phoḍle āhā; visni ghetle āhā
nāngracyā tayāryā apūn setavariyā rahalyā āhā;
hālse dongari halsānā; pātcidongari (pāti) ānāyā jāyjā;
lavange sutār bolavlā; kunbyālā kusā lohārāce darī;
lohārdādā tuji kāmā rahu des mālā kusā tayār karun dijos.

rokḍā dām cukavlā chālālyā lāglā āhā;
tasa yo nangracha mirghacha pani padaya lagla aha;
calā jav nāngrā jupāyā jā koṭi holāvar parayānayā karāyā;
yek ṭakkā paryānā kelyā āhā;
setivarā perayun rikāmi zāli āhā
ye holā ukhalāyā lāgli āhā;
tasyā holā ukhalūn rikāmī calā jāv māḍi māhalāt
jāv āpun nāngar māngāyā
sāt disānce peryānyā zālyā hotyā;
te hūn bhāt vādhāyā don pānā vādhun cār pānā vādhun pāca
pānā vādhūn ālī āhā.
kunbī lāgle bolāyā pāni nāhi sonā pāḍā
jāmboṭice cikhal karja;
bhāt khanāyā lāgli āhā kunbi ta lāgli āhā khanāyā;
māṭh bhājicā maḍā sāt mādā ghetalī āhā;
sirdhicā sarahāta sāt māḍā ghetalā āhā;
pahali hoti rābkarin mangā āli mālāt ātā zāli mālkarī;
yekekāli don kāḍiya vāḍhun dijos
yek thobī don thombī dijos
māl kliyāl jāyajos
doghā kunbi ābun hātāt khuḍjos hātāt khudjos
nako vaḍtī hoyjos;
jasā kalniyā samīdar vādhun ālā tase tu tar vaḍhun vijos;
tase ambunā rīkāmī zalī āhā,
akhāḍ mahinā vartun gelā, sarāvan ugavlā,
sarāvan vartun gelā bhādavā mahinā ungūn ālā;
bhātā hoti garbī zāli bhātā nisavun paḍlī
khālace mārgālā ānalī āhā,
hivān mahani nāhi khāli pasant zāli,
tāmbaḍ māti nighun gelī
nāhi khāni chintā mani murum malīlā nighun gelī
nāhi khāli pasant zāli udār mānelā;
tatha khali pasant keli; atha khālā fār barā; udār āhā
sātse kamārila hākā mārlyā chalā kamāriho khalī khurpā
khālpason khurpāyā lāgli āhā; yekāc
disālā khalā khurpun rikāmi zāli āhā

gāyācī sina keli āhā; sārvan kelā āhā;
ātā bhātā kāpāyā lāgli āhā,
uḍviyavar uḍvācevar bharjos bhātā rikāmī zāle,
pus mahinā ugavalā āhā,
loṭiyāce dukāni agarbatti punjāyā ānjos,
nārlāce punjā ānjos;
tevahu punjā ghetli āhā, mādi māhali gelā āhā,
bhagtālā atha rākhunbiyā tu koṭha jās,
masālā vaḍhit kāmā āhā,
cal dādā sānce pāhanālā yet āhā;
sānce pāharālā ālā āhā vāḍesar,
basalā āhā; tambākhu ghetlā āhā
viḍyā vālalyā āhā; viḍyā tāna āhā;
vidyā toḍlyāt āhā
hāt dhovale āhā
pāy dhovla āhā;
bārā jān vādit jān khāmbāsi basālā āhā;
pānglāice nāvāce kunḍal ṭhevle āhā;
uḍvesi dādā tasī oḍhun vadhalī āhā;
khāmbasi neli āhā
jānghevar ḍāve pāyāce ghetle āhā;
pahalyā dhaḍyā silkil khāndi karjos;
bhārela muḍā nā karjos
asī hi hālpet tasī vādel hoijos;
tū jasā durug vāḍhun ālā tasā pāngālāy vaḍhun mī jos;
nārliche vāḍit chadtiyā hoti, usāce vayāt caḍti hotī
dhānice mulacyā, khadoice kolhācā,
dodkiyācyā vaḍyāt cāngalyā hotyā;
mānḍe pāyeisī pāy muhal ānī koparāpāsi hāt muhal;
tuze karitā jīv mārun,
ajagīnā dagā phaṭkā karajā nako
kunbilā suṭi dijos;
yā dādā dupālalyā mangā cāri khanḍālā
johārlyā mangā dhaḍā khāmbet bharli āhā;
malnī suruvāt zāli, zoḍnī suruvāt,
malā bhātācā tāngaḍ bharāyācā

dhānāchyā goni lasanācyā goni bharāyacyā;
yā malanyā cālalyā āhā, dhigā kunbi geli āhā saharāle
dhānācyā mulicyā kāceca usācyā kathyā ghetlyā āhā,
keliche longrā ghetli āhā,
geli nighun loṭiche dukānāvar geli āhā;
ṭicakī bāngdi kāli gāthi, āichā sāmān ghyāyālā gavali
kāchi divā lāvāyā kaḍvā tel goḍā tel, ghetlā āhā,
loḍe mārge bāri vānī var nighun āli,
ātā nighun tar bhagat ālā āhā;
āicā upās to doghā kunbi rahali āhā;
sānjece pāharālā nighun ta kansari mātā
(panglai) reshmā kumār zaltī kelī
kājalā kumār jaltī kelī
nārandeva hirobādeva mahuvari kovā ghetlā āhā;
nighun var cālalyā sanjān saarālā
borḍet saarālā rātice paḍvyālā
konivār gelā kāy;
kālā kālī hātālā luli hotī; pāyālā nevri hotī;
kāloicā loṭṇāt milocā purjyā ticyā
mukhadācā asād kelyā hotyā
dhāvlāca ghānghali kelyā;
tase borḍe saarāsī dahānu saarālā
hirobā deva murumbābā vājvat jāy;
nāran deva moḍamode nācat jāy;
tasi pānglāy sadmā deva sadma karun
rāgāce rātri kunbyāce pāṭh soḍun
pot soḍun jāyā lāgli;
kunbi hotā hālāt paḍlā; tuzi dasā phār dur geli āhā;
vāāngaon sahar, hirobā deva mārgālā lāglā;
nāran yo āyelā mānapāya jāt āhā
tarī pan tuzevar hāy hāy kunbyā.
nābhu (bhivu nako) nāko bhije; sani boltā patkaralyā;
nābhu mardā tuzi dasā phār dur geli āhā jāt āhā;
mhanun tuze kartā jivmār jivtār;
upās kar; gāyicā gorhā kuṭun mār;
don goṭhāvā dharti toḍli dharticā pānī
kelā ase tuje hāl ara kasā kelā

rin kelā chin kelā
pālghar saharālā āicā pattā nāhi lāgat āhā;
kelve saharālā yevade mārgālā āhā;
kelve shaharālā kelice pātilā
dasāvi hinḍat hoti;
dhar bāi kelici longra din tuze
keli din tuje keli nāy ghin dāsā palāli āhā;
dādar saharālā hinḍat jāeen ṭhāne saharālā ujavi kālāli;
humay device nighun geli; tatha himāi deva bolāyā lagli;
tujā tāngad mālā dijo; tāngaḍ cālāyā lāglā āhā;
tuji dāsā vāroli saharālā
tatha tāngaḍni neya lāgli āhā;
rem bharambe geli ghin nāngar hi dāsā nāgvi āhā;
tuji dasā pālavali kāli gāthi agalit āhā;
ḍāvyā hātāt bāngḍyā āhā;
tyāvar tu hāt tākjos;
nāy neyāci malā lāthan mārla āhā;
supākhal mārlā āhā, māzā kān tutalā āhā;
muslākhan mārala āhā;
māzā dāt paḍle āhā; bhārikhal mārle āhā;
māzā kān toḍlā āhā;
bhārākhāl mārale āhā, zodli toḍli āhā
mag hiravā deva māhāvari havā vājvāyā lāglā āhā;
nāran deva moramoḍi nācāyā lāglā āhā;
tasī amāl pānglāy mānavli āhā;
tasi ghāngli bājāyā tayār zālā,
goni vanjārā sātse goni tayār karjo;
save vanjārā sive vanjārā tehe
vanjārā goni bharāyā kelicyā
goni bharāyā lāglā
dhānicyā goṇi mulicyā goni nārlācyā goni
bharāyā lāglyā;
hāke vanjār bāre vanjārā tāngaḍ bhar;
sātse tāngaḍ bharāyā laglyā; āyecā tāngaḍ rām bharābi;
tasi pānglāyāice tāngadāranāryā dādā;
māzā kunbi hālāt paḍal chākari karal ughḍā pāni paḍat nāhi;
cala bāy phār barā tujā kunbi sevā karat āhā

āichyā tāngḍāt basali āhā rembharombhi
karnāli saharālā ālā tāngaḍ rembharombhi,
tyācyā gālyālā bara mbhovācā deva
ādāvā phiralā nāngatāici dasā;
jāt āhā tujā bāy jānāyinā koth pāḍlā
mī bāy kosbād gāvāt māzā kunbi hālāt āhā,
varsā kurāvat karāyā jāt āhā
melechā jitā karan thotyācā dhaḍā karan;
tasā tāngaḍ vālat ān
māngat māngat gheun yet pānde nāḍ ghet yet
tasā tāngaḍ sāt samīndar ādavā paḍlā;
ṭāke dādālā hākā mārlyā;
tāke dādā tāran ānjos māzā tāngaḍ devāun dijos;
ye tāru devārun dijos;
he tāru devārun dijos rokaḍ don dilyā chukun;
hāke vanjārā bombe vanjārā bombā ṭhokā
tasā tangaḍ devā lāglā;
sāvaṭe sahari māge naḍ (jāt) panḍe nāḍ pāḍ ghet jāt;
āyi māze re bharosi thepthepi āichā
tāngaḍ; rami chānd mata āḍvi paḍli;
ubhā kelī hi pāgal āhā jātā yetā kothe paḍli?
talavli saharālā ālat tasā tāngaḍ tech kālālā;
tasā tāngaḍ rembharobi;
kunbi jagsuj zāli tuzā tāngaḍ yet āhā;
yi tāngaḍ devāve lohe mārge ghānekar saharāt nighun ālā;
mori candōbā āḍvā paḍlā;
yehi sadmā keli cāvlācā ghāngal kelā;
kolashyācā puār kelā nilisicā pan kelā
ye koḍica pun kelā;
mukhācyā asādyā kelyā āhā;
māzā kunbi māzi sevā karākā nāhi?
sadmā karun mi jāt āhā;
tasi sosat lohe mārge hāke vanjārā bobevanjārā
bombā mārat āhā;
tārpe vanjārā ghāgare vanjārā tāngaḍ rembharombi rahan ān
tasā tāngaḍ devāyā lāglā; boroḍe saharāsi devāyā lāglā;
gāvācā devā āḍvā paḍlā teth tāngaḍ ubhā kelā;

yidādā pānglāy pāynicā pān kelā
bāsing painicā bāsing keli
tanoḍā sati zāle; sapti zāli;
kosbāḍ gāvāt didole holāt tāngaḍ ālā pujice holāt;
hāy hāy kunbyā nābhu mardā nako bhijo;
sani budhlā pāhtarālā khulnāce dhigāsi;
khalyāche tāngaḍ ālā; ye tāngaḍ kunbilā thepālat hinḍā;
tasā tāngaḍ soniyāche khānbasi loṭun ṭāklā;
tyācyā maga rasi kelyā;
ḍodkicyā vāḍyā kohalyācyā vaḍyā
usācyā vaḍyā cādyā kelyā;
dhānachyā chānḍyā kelyā;
haldicyā vaḍyā āicyā lagna nācholi pānā zāli;
tasī mangā rembharobi ṭhepoṭhepi bāgān bhāve khāli lāgle;
ye tāngaḍ vādtā karun melichā dhajā
karun thotichā jitā karun
bārā vāḍyā punjā keli;
vārli āravat kombḍi punjā keli;
soni āḍalyā kunbin āg ho lagli
bārā vāgila āj suṭi dijos;
ye kunbilā suṭi dijos;
saglyānci pinyāci dagā phaṭkā kāhi karjos nako
varsī (pāus) purāvā karjos. (See app. 3.1)

(Tr. : As the story goes the farmers went to the Parsi landlord, whose land was situated in the jambudni rivulet. This land was unprepared, hence, they had to look at the fields, and they liked them and went to see the landlord. The land was granted to them by him. In the evening they had food with the caretaker and discussed their requirements. About seven hundred workers were needed.

The farmers went to Ganjan in search of workers and from thence to Bordi, to a Vadwal, (farmer), who asked them where they were going. "We have come to search for seven hundred workers for our land", they replied. The Vadval told them that the workers were in the plantations and that there were no workers available. From here, the farmers went to Wangaon, but without success, had to proceed to Boiser and from there to Palaghar. They asked a trader (vāṇī) but the workers were employed in a factory. The farmers were now in trouble. They visited the kingdom of the lame, and the Rui and worshipped the Rui tree that had withered. They had no success. They proceeded to Shirgaon and saw blossoms and also noticed the workers. They filled their baskets and got ready to start for the new land in the early hours of the morning with their families. They crossed the hills and descended with the winds from the sea, towards the hills of Jawar. Their lips were perched and stomachs empty, the young and the old met each other and descended to Talvada...Vetti...and Gholvad, than to Kosbad.

They rested at Manor and drank āmbil (fermented drink from the flour...). They slept for the night. Next morning they demanded that their instruments be sharpened. They visited the black-smith at Manor and then visited the forests and found that the sāag, āin and other trees had withered. From here they went to the Mushi Hills and were not satisfied with the forest of Hindoli and Maholi Hills. The two farmers went to the Caali Hills which were dense with plenty of trees. Here they met a fakīr. They offered a coconut, lead powder and some bracelets and then returned under the shade of the thick forests. The seven hundred workers were told to get ready their food for fifteen days, to begin cutting the forests where the wind god is worshipped with shendoor (lead powder), coconuts, cock, etc.

Now they began to cut the forests day by day, trees fell, for fifteen days, and then descended to the rivulet and rested. When the sun rose, and when its rays reached on the earth, they woke up and taking their instruments began to make bunds on the Jambudni river as well as on the kumbutti river. This work went on till the beginning of June. The clouds were seen in the sky and the first monsoon was on the way. There was thundering and the farmer looked towards the east and shouted at the workers to assemble and prepare for the rāab...the rains poured.

The farmer sent his wife Pateri to the loft, to see some seeds, kudai, har-kudai, beans, tur, ambadi, nagli, vari etc...but she did not find any. So they decide, to go to the landlord (Parsi), he too had no seeds for them. The woman than went to the king...but he too had no seeds worthwhile... They ask the Gongeri, the mungli...but finally they approach the trader (vāṇī) who gave them the needed seeds.

The twelve leaders proclaimed that the seeds are taken to the new lands. The young bulls were tied to the sãag tree and their nostrils were pierced and they got ready for the ploughing. The plough blades was sharpened by the iron-smith and ready cash was paid to him. "The rains have started, lets get ready to plough, lets sow the seeds, the fields are ready now, lets watch from our huts. The sowing is over in seven days." The seedlings sprouted. The rivers were flowing and it is raining gold from the heavens (meaning good rain), lets go now and puddle the fields. The seedlings were now plucked and the weeds like mãat and with other woods removed from the *rãab*, the seedlings were taken to the fields and transplanted sparingly two by two, they help the planters who are tired.

The farmers shout "keep on planting and cover the ground like the receding tides." The ploughing is now over. It was the month of August, and September was near. The late varieties were flowering and getting ready and were on the way to the threshing floor.

The floor, the red-mud floor, the murum floor was not chosen but the plot of land that was not used was chosen for the threshing floor. All the workers were employed and the floor was ready within a day. The floor was smeared with cow dung. The paddy meanwhile was being cut, the sheaves were arranged in a ring on the floor. It was the cold month of January...was the time of the blessing and the feast of the *rãas*. The coconut and the *agarbatis* were ready for the *puja*. The Bhagat was invited but he refused saying he had plenty of work. He was ready to come by evening. The farmer agreed. He came and they all sat on the threshing floor. At the center pole in the *khala* small heaps of rice were kept in the name of the Vanglava deva. A sheaf of the new paddy is pulled out from the heap and placed near the left foot of the Bhagat, and at the center pole. Firstly, get ready to send the Kansari to the Shilkhand, go round the *khala* with the winnowing fan and ask for the blessings. The coconut, the sugarcane, the vegetables like the coriander, radish, onions, mash-malon, pumpkin etc., are in plenty. The sheaf is put on the center pole (*khal med*). The *malnī* is on and the farmers have gone to the market to buy some coriander, onions, sugarcane, plantains (for the ceremony,) black bangles, gathi, some bitter oil for the lamp and they return. The Bhagat anxiously waits for them. The farmer and the wife fast for this occasion. The gods Kansari, Panglia, Rashmai kumar, Kazla kumar, Naran deva, Hiroba deva, Mahori dave are moving towards Sanjan, the Maloshi flows into the Kaloshi river at the ashad (on the boundary of Talasiri taluk). The farmer suffered his fate. He was assured that his sufferings would be over soon, if he prayed and did penance.

The goddess Kansari was angry because the farmer had killed a bull and she left the earth in tears behind her. She left for Palaghar town and from there to Kelva, there she roamed the plantations. She was offered by the Kunbi (farmer) plantains but she refused and went to Daddra via Thane. There the angry Kansari met Humai God, who said to the kunbi (farmer) "Give me your *tāngad* (the instrument for his working well) and your dāsī (kansari) is filled with the milk, she wears a black *gāthī*, and bangles on the left hand. Go and put a garland around her".

The goddess Kansari refused saying that "I have been ill-treated. They have put under foot my head my bead necklace and beaten me with the winnowing fan, plucked my ears and struck me with a pounding rod and knocked my teeth off. They have struck me with a broom and broken my ringlets and anklets." Then the Hirobā and Vāran joked at her and then the Kansari was pleased and the *gānglī* player and the *duff* player got ready. The sack merchant got ready the seven hundred sacks. The fillers, the pressers, the stitchers, got ready. They filled the sacks with plantains, coconuts etc...they filled the *tāngad* (pots) too.

The farmer (a general representative of farmers) requests the Kansari to return saying that his fellow farmer (at whose house the *rāas* ceremony is to be done) is a good man, an honest fellow, who serves you faithfully. There is no rain, he is disturbed, he needs you. The Kansari goddess forgives and with the *tāngad* pot has come to Karnali swiftly and the lord Barambha looked behind and found the mother Kansari in trouble. Where are you going? She replied "My farmer brother is in trouble and I am going to help him out. I will raise the dead and heal the lame. I will take the *tāngad* to assist him. The guides will help me to cross the seven seas. She called out to the boatman, "please bring the boat" and take the *tāngad* across the sea. Two boat men were available. They thus reached the Savta creek (near Dahanu).

It was getting dark and the moon peeped out from the clouds and the heavens protected the *tāngad* (sacred) and they reached Talavali and the group descended the hills and came to Chanaghar and the moon shone brightly. They all bowed to it and offered rice and invoked the gods of Kālosī, Nilosī. They sang and played the *Tārpā* and came to Boronda. The village god (Wāghya) stopped them but they offered him flowers, plantains and proceeded across the rivers Dudhola and Pujola to the village of Kosbad, towards the *khala*, to be blessed. "Oh farmer of ours don't be afraid the bird *shannibudia* is sitting besides the *khorsani* heap. The *tāngad* (gods instrument) has come to your *khala*" and they go round the *khala* heaps. The threshed paddy was heaped and the vegetables were kept beside (the pumpkin mashmelon, sugarcane, turmeric, radish, etc.) and all rejoiced at the Knsari wedding. The Bhagat began his zun danic (possessed). The dead will live and the lame will walk. A young cock was offered and the housewife made the aarti and prayed to the goddess Kansari "protect O goddess, the workers, and the household members from all evil and grant us good rain in the coming year".)

The word kansari is used by the farmer of Thane district for paddy or *kanis*. The Warlis cultivating the low lands normally grow rice and therefore to them Kansari means the paddy. The high landers cultivating the slopes of the hills normally grow *nāglī* and *vārī*. The *nāglī* grain is considered to be important and Kansari is related to it. This grain is small, dark in color, and is considered to be very nutrious and sturdy. At the time of the sowing the farmers give special respect to the grain and then follow some kind of fast and abstention from drinks and from certain vegetables like mula, plantains, kakdi etc.

At the end of the harvest a special *pujā* is performed by the farmers by calling the Gangli Bhagat and an assistant, zun Bhagat. The *gāngali* is a special musical instrument with two pumpkins with a bamboo rod and two wires (*dutārī*). The Bhagats sing the Kansari khand in praise of the goddess which is lame and has tremendous power. To offend the goddess is considered a big offence and may lead to a bad crop and even starvation. Hence the farmers make it a point to placate the deity even if it means expenditure.

The goddess Kansari is known to be dark in colour, short, lame and not very pretty. She is called by some Warlis as *pāngal āi*, a lame mother. Nobody knows the reason for her lameness. Some time after the harvest the farmer and his wife who have kept the fast invite their friends to the khala. A heap of nagli grain is made before the *med*, a lamp is lit, the Bhagat sits in front of the *med* with the household and the zun Bhagat. The Bhagat then makes rice *punjali* (heaps) in front of the *med* and chants his khands in praise of the kansari. The offerings of mula, sugarcane, a plantain, *kohalā*, and coconut is kept around the heap of grain. After the *pujā* the Bhagat instructs the farmers wife by offering her a handful of grains and telling her that she is responsible for the use of the grain and therefore must feed the household judiciously and make good use of the Kansari. The zun Bhagat who gets possessed becomes stiff and cannot walk, his legs get crouched and begins to move only on his seat. As a sign that the lame Kansari goddess has entered possessed him, he begins to complain about the ill-treatment by the farmer for burning her, abusing her, not being generous with those in need of grains, etc. It appears that the burning implies the roasting of the bread. The Warlis say that it was not, in their tradition to bake the bread on both sides in early days as this meant that were burning the Kansari. This is the reason why the zun Bhagat states that he was burnt, lashed and maltreated. The housewife resembles the Kansari goddess, hence any ill treatment meted out to her by the husband is considered an offence to the Kansari goddess. The Kansari goddess through the zun Bhagat asks the main Bhagat whether there is the sacrifice of a black cock and a chicken, and black goat and another goat for placation. Once the Bhagat says yes, the Kansari goddess leaves the *zun* Bhagat and people stretch his hands and feet and make him stand. The goats are killed one in the name of the Kansari goddess and the other in the name of other Gods. Then the chicken is roasted and kept hanging on the *palād* till the next day to be consumed in the morning by the family.

Chapter 4

The Ritu-Cakra

The Warli calender is seasonal, and revolves around from *ākhād* to *ākhād*. The advent of the month of May sees the Warlis living on *āmbīl* (porridge from *jowār* or *nāglī* flour). People look emancipated, sick and tired due to hard labour in the nearby towns and poor food at home. The cattle too is weak due to lack of fodder and water. The huts look deserted and are badly kept. The forest too is dry and looks thin. Several children suffer from water borne diseases. The old are left to themselves. Several Warlis go in search of paddy seeds, bullocks for ploughing and money for the coming agricultural operations.

Getting Ready For Sowing

The seeds are blessed. The Bhagat lights a lamp, prays to the gods and the house-holder touches the feet of the Bhagat. One onion is put in the basket till the sowing is over. The husband-wife duo then keep the *pāl*, abstain from certain vegetables.

Ropnī

Once the new paddy seedlings are ready, the house-holder himself plants the *sindi*, *mat*, *bhājī* and *dab* (green grass). He prays "from the gush of winds, the rains and in the name of the soil, I am leaving the seeds in the earth, protect it oh god from the birds and insects, from pests and diseases and let it grow well".

Panachivā

The Bhagats carry the flowers of *jowar*, *makhaā*, paddy, chilly, and keep on the ant hill with some eggs and milk and liquour and than offer it to the mother earth.

Kolī Bhajī

Warlis get their vegetables during the first rains. They are cooked by the Warlis and eaten together with the family. Small heaps of rice (*punjali*) along with some *kolī* vegetables are kept, the light is lit. Some liqor is poured. All the members of the household sit and eat. All of them take some liquor.

Ghad Bāndhnē

On the *khala*, a pile is made at the center with the sheaf of paddy stock upside down on the top of the pole. This ritual is done before the threshing begins.

Malnī

Malnī literally means the threshing operation, which starts at the end of the November and continues through out the December. The Kansari *pujā* is observed after *malnī* in the month of *Kartik* or *Margasira*. The *Reval* is done in the field for Kansari *mātā*, the black one. Bhagat, the "wise-man" performs the Kansari *pujā* during the *malnī* in the open field late in the evening.

Wāghobā

October—November Twelfth day of the second fortnight of the *Kārtik* about two days before Divali, Wāghobā (a tiger god) is seen on the outskirt of the village. He is depicted in a wooden stump with a carving of a tiger figure.

Navā Bhāt

Pohe are made of the new paddy. One grain is kept on the leaf of *Denī* plant. This is meant for the *pujā*. With the sheaf of paddy, mango leaves and wild paddy grass a garland is made out on the main door, or on the main pillar of the house (*Mēd Bhāal*) and is marked by a sendoor *tillā*. Then the rest of the ceremony follows.

Dussera

The *āvāz* is played during the night, the songs of the god Hanum are sung.

Divāli Bāras

About a weak before *Divālī* the villagers and Bhagat go to the hill and put up a small hut, (*palād*) for the night vigil. Zun trance dance is performed by the Bhagats and flowers, a sack of new rice paddy and a new white cloth is offered. They dance the whole night at the *pintha*, a place prepared on the hill. Two Bhagats give *tillā* to gods, carry the *Chol*, *math*, *sendoor*, chicken (cock), coconut, flowers. Whole *cavalī* pods, *tikā*, and bangles are offered. They then come down in the morning, put together the gifts, eat and drink, meet each other and go home. The *āaratī* is made by the lady of the house and it is understood that the crop will be good. A good *hālphā* (crop) is expected.

Pitribāras

In August-September, *Bhādrapad* on the 12th day of the IInd fortnight of *Bhādrapad*, a big *melā*-(*yātrā a gathering*) is held in a Mahalaxmi temple near Charoti. New Bhagats and his students are initiated. *Pujā* is performed to the tree (*aptā* tree). A coconut is broken and offering is made and the *navas* (*row*) made.

Divālī

For Warlis, *Divālī* is a festival to remember the family gods which are generally kept with the main family of the clan. These family gods are known as *garcā deva* which are carefully kept in a basket of a particular shape. During the time of *Divālī* the icons of the family gods are washed with milk and are worshipped by the household head.

Makara Sankrānt

Unlike the larger society, Warlis observe the festivity of *makara* sankrānt by conducting hunting and fishing expedition. Male members as a matter of convention go to the deep forest in search of games and never return back empty handed. The women prefer to go to streams and enjoy their day catching fish. Both the male and female groups come back in the dusk, jumping and singing merrily in anticipation of a good meal in the evening.

Shimgā

The ceremony of *shimgā* resembles hōlī of sanskritised communities. They observe this occasion with a bounty of nostalgic pleasure and often get drunk which leads to fights among themselves.

Devāce Lagna (Gāv Deva)

Somewhere in the second week of December every village celebrates its *gāra deva*. Different villages have their own deva. Some keep the *Wāghis deva*, the lord of the jungles. He protects the village and its cattle. Some choose *Rānī Rāi* cā Wāghoba and some others *cānd mātā*. A *pujārī* and the elders of the village take the contributions from the hamlets according to the *Nāngar* (plough). The *pujārī* buys six coconuts, sendoor, sweet oil and some bitter oil (kado tel). The day for the *pujā* is fixed and all members of the hamlet gather round the deity somewhere at the outskirts of the village. A goat or a pig is brought along with a cock for the five headed Chedda.

The Tornī Chedda

Two poles at the entrance of the village with a line of mango leaves and flowers is a common feature in every village, which guards the village from the evil spirits. Any one passing from this chedda is reminded that he should leave behind their evil spirits, and the seven evil spirits are believed to keep off from the village.

The Bhagat with two helpers sit round the deity and begin his chants. No woman takes part in this ceremony. The chants continue for the whole night. Three *dattas* (small drums) are kept near the ankle and played with a stick, while the chants center around the nature, the sun, the earth and *dharna kori*. The different chedda, (small posts outside, village on fields etc). Torni chedda, Nakhari chedda, Godi chedda (stone figure) Mahari chedda etc., are more probably the names of the past *gurūs* from whom the art of the Bhagats is learnt. Every clan seems to have its own *gurū*. Thus we hear about the god Mahdar, Namta, Namin, Kakdia, Gura, Lakhma, Sutar, Tokre, Madhar, Vadga Madhar (guru) which suggest a long existing tradition where the wise-man has been playing an important role.

The chant mentions the names of important rivers. It is called the *Sore* Chant... The Sore is the dirt from the body of the Goddess Gauri and its stream (sore over) flows along the slopes (Mani) of Kasar, Shival, Kowali, Dapsi then to Gondali man and Rohadi man.

These then flow along the hills and the chant mentions them by names Bhavarkdada, Nimbhala, Chotval, Hindoli, Khindoli, Maholi, Rasi durung (at Mahalaxmi) Pokdia durung (hill) at present Kurke, Gambhir gad at Ude, Kna at Mogaon Barda at Gangangao, Bhuighat at Damangao and Kamba kore at Bhandaara (At Ambat sari—bari). These are the hills where a daughter of a Bhandari took refuge. Mushia dorigar (the peak at the Mahalaxmi) and other near by hills; Kumbia, Ghat, Vag, Dava, Ashari, Chamak etc., find a place in the narration.

After chanting the prayers the villagers are then mentioned, from where the brahmana descends to the marriage pendal. The Dhavleri (marriage priestess) reciets this song. The Bhagat then chants the chant of Annach Bheiss.

mohor chal bakrice tand...yocna re deva.
pilad kar (amount) magarsi ale
gai ce re tanda yocnā re deva.
Gaivar pilan kar...magarshī ale gogo (calfs)
gomr hrla yocāna re deva.
Vag jalmala dȧkhina jala. (in boat)...yocna re deva...
pilan kar bayal zav...yudi re deva satta kodhe gelī
vesa khothe gelī (spirits).

(Tr. Go ahead o shepherd, mount from behind. Cow herd mount on the cow as the calf follows. Mount on the bull, where is your rule, where have the spirits gone.)

The musical instrument kahali (shenai) are played to the Warli traditional tunes. The Bhagats and some elders get possessed with the spirit, and do a wild dance. The two helpers sitting beside the deity take a pot of water and put some rice into it. This floating rice is distributed to the farmers present. This is called the *Hafta*.

These grains are taken to the threshing floor and kept in the heaps of paddy sheaves.

The goat which quietly watches these ceremonies waits for the final fatal blow from the axe. The goat is struck with a sickle behind the neck and killed preferable with one stroke. The blood of the animal is then smeared on the floor, to placate the ancestral gods.

The goat offering now is taken aside and roasted on the slow fire to remove hair etc. Small pieces are made, and distributed to the householders who have made the contribution. This meat is cooked at home and then a good meal is enjoyed by all the members of the household. The Bhagat is given his share too.

With this feast the Warlis are free to do other feasts and family celebrations. From now onwards Warlis observe different festivities in the village and dance to the tune of the *kahali* and the dhol. As mentioned elsewhere, beside the evil spirits the Warlis placate, the good spirits are also invoked. Hence in the preceding chant, the Bhagat complains to god of the evil and the injustice that haunts the village.

Hirva Ihu (Garab/Garbha)

Hirva is a clan god kept in the house of the elder of the clan and placated once a year and is kept inside a basket called salad. The image of Hirva is placed on the floor of the house. A square drawing of rice is made with two diagonal lines.

The main Bhagat sits in front of the deity with three assistant chanters who sit behind him with the small drums on their anklets (dhakas). The chant follows :

Ihu or Hirva Chant

The wife of Hiran Garjia says :
padālā janmā yāchā pursa don jevanārā;
chul peṭav ātā tū khā
āni mālā pan de, mi moṭhā deva chūl peṭvat nāhi.
Aag phukūn tar
māzyā mishā peṭatil. veḍā bāgḍā tu chūl

peṭav āni jevana rānd.
chul peṭavlyā āni jevnā rāndhli.
Pāca divsācā padar hotā to
māvloon gelā, tāmbyāt ghaḍ ghetlā, raj bāvilā nighoon geli,
kāsar mānila nighoon geli;
māti nāngāyā māti pasant nāhi zāli
chikoon mātila valali; khalpyā kelyā; matyā kadalyā
kholi māti neyin tar malā bar hoyil
āni kholyā asā kān hoti
dudit mātyā neyin tar dudyā asā poṭ hoyil
mangā cālāya lāgli palsācyā buḍāsi,
nighun geli tetha virāl
soḍun thevlā. palsāci phoola tambḍi zāli.
savricyā buḍāsī nighoon geli, tatha viṭāl soḍun ṭhevli;
sāvrici phula tāmbadī zāli. odyācā velisi nighun
geli tyāci phula rāti zāli.
Vāhatī gangālā nighoon geli. muriāde pānī geli
girbhāchi choli dhārilā ṭhevli, devān sāḍi dhārilā ṭhevli.
māvḍyā odit pānyāt geli, mandyā bhijavlyā,
māthi bhijavalyā; māthi budavayā;
māti cholali; padar vāhatyā
ganget soḍun ṭhevlā; musācā masālā padar zeloon ghetlā;
oli soḍli korḍi lāvli; rāj bāvilā nighoon gelī.
ghaḍā cholalā, malālā, pāni bharlā, lohoṭe mārgi,
maḍi māhali
ghara āli agrai nigri bhātā keli
purusālā hākā mārlyā, soni tāti jevnā vādhali.
devān jevan vādhalā mag muravi malalā
sodalā ghāsālā jevālā; basalā.
andheri kholi nighun gelā.
soneri palangā nijlā. andheri rātche
caḍāvadi karu lāglā; nār hoti tā goṅdhalun geli
jevan nāy bhāva; pānī nāy bhāva;
poṭichā bāman ālā bolu lāglā; tujyā poṭāt garaba hāe.
garabha vāḍhu lāglā, ek, mahinā zālā, don, tin...
nava mahini zāle, nava velā, nava dis, nava ghaṭkā;
nava tās

poṭ dukhu lāglā...ihulā hākā mārlyā...
loṭyācyā dukānāt gelā
bārā suyā ghetlyā. gajarāice hātāt dilyā
tu tar gnadā suḍkā kāy shivāyā ānlās.
sevṭi saharālā nighoon gelā
suvin ānli hātāt ghetli lākdi. suyin bārā beloti āli
gāyice goṭhani nigoon geli. gāy gābhan hoti.
veyu lāgli ḍokri mājā hoḍ kar.
tujyā singā kādsi tar shingā mārasi,
pāya kādasi tar pāyān
mārse, tujā bāl tūch sinajos; dharti pāḍjos;
chātoon choomboon cāltā karjos.
maḍi māhali nighoon geli ukharḍi ḍhigavar kombḍi carat hote
ti bolāyā lāglī; ḍokri jās koth? ekāci dogha karāyā jāy
kombḍilā boloo lāgli tujyā poṭilā hāḍ jalmal...gharāt geli bāi paḍun hoti
poṭāt dukhat hota talālā tel lāvlā
āḍvā bāl cānglā gelā, bāi bālāntan zāli dhartivar bāl paḍlā
nāl bāndhali kacyā sutāvar
boravāci sāli kāḍhali, nāl kāpalā
var dāṭali, deva dhartīvar paḍalā (See app. 4.1)

(Tr. : The wife of God Hirva...Garija says "I have my periods today, go and cook food for me and for you". The Lord replied, "I am the Lord, and I will not cook. If I blow the fire my moustache may burn." But the wife demanded and the Lord at last agreed and cooked food somehow. The five day period was over and Garija went to the stream. She saw the mud on the bank, but it did not please her, she saw the dry sticky scalps of mud and she said to herself, "If I take the scalps my child will have the ears like the plantain leaf. If I take the mud in big pots my child will have a pot belly".

She went to the palas tree and due to her menses, the flowers of the tree become red, she went to the cotton tree, and flowers turn red. She went to odila creeper and its root turned reddish. Then she went to the river ankle deep, she kept her blouse and sari at the side, she went knee deep and washed her head and hair rubbed them and scrubbed them, the fishes nibbled at her clothes. She changed from the wet clothes into dry ones. Then she went to the palace wall, she scrubbed the pots and washed them and filled them with clean water. Returned home and cooked food, a simple meal of dal and rice. She call her husband and serves his meal in a golden plate. He ate and was filled. Rose up and went to his room and slept on the golden bed. He was restless and at midnight he had intercourse. His wife Garija was disturbed because she would be pregnant she did not eat nor drink until she was told that she would be a mother. A Brahmin confirmed it. She was happy. The months passed till the ninth month...nine days passed...nine intervals...nine hours and the time had come. The husband went to the market and bought nine needles... Garjia rebuked him, "do you intend to stitch a blanket?" The husband went to town to look for a nurse and the nurse crossing the road with twelve junctions came to the village. She entered the stable. A cow requested her to help her in the delivery. The old woman said if I go to your tail, you will kick me, if I go the head you will buck me. You manage yourself. The calf was born and the mother cow licked and cleaned and the young calf walked. She came to the dung-hill and saw a hen foraging. The hen asked the old woman "Where are you going?" "I am going to separate the two and make them one each. You will give birth to a bone (egg)", she replied.

The nurse reached Garijas house who was in labor and pain. She applied oil to her hands and helped in the delivery. The baby was born. The umbilical cord was tied with a raw thread and cut by a reed, stripped and was buried. Thus the god was born on this earth.

Kādicā Deva

This ceremony is done when there is pestilence on the crops etc... When some pest is suspected on crops the villagers gather together and perform the puja in a chosen house. All the farmers bring along some wet mud and make images of the insects like grass-hoppers, caterpillars, rats, rabbits, etc., and spray them with shendoor powder, dhum (incense), a coconut is broken and water is sprinkled around the images. A group of farmers and women sing and dance around the main pole of the house where a lamp is lit and kept hanging from the pillar. The Bhagats meanwhile keep on chanting the prayers asking the gods 'protection on the crop'. The dance in the house goes on sometimes for the whole night. Early in the morning a cock is cut and then taken to the Bhagats, and served with liquor. The mud images are then taken in a cup, a winnowing fan and thrown into the nearest river. This whole ceremony begins late in the evening and finishes early in the morning. No drums are used for this *Devnaca the* dance of the gods. Only men folk dance with some balls round the ankle. The male folk sing and the women sitting in the corner of the house repeat after them.

Dance for Nāran Deva

During the time of *Kolī* and *Navā* eating, the men folk gather in a house where the promise to god Nāran is made to protect the family from evil. Hence this dance is not done by all in the village. A lamp is lit and kept on the main pole of the house in the center. The dancers sing and the women respond to the tune. A *dolak* sits in the middle and with the sounds of the tiny balls they sing merrily, often through the night. If no rains come for some days, this dance goes on for five days.

Gāvri Dance

Some young men and women take part in this dance usually done every night after Monsoon and before the harvest. Some of the men tie small balls to their ankles, a drummer sits in the center. The men folk sing and the women reply. There is a mood of happiness since the harvest is near and several of them have sufficient earlier variety of paddy to feast upon. This dancing begins after the *nāgpancamī* till the end of Gaṇapatī festival. The songs donot seem to be from the Warli tradition, but are taken from the neighbours.

Holi Festival

Several days before the actual Holi, little Warli children gather together in the village square and celebrate in their simple ways the *kāmbad* holi. They dance round the fire, shout abuses etc. The actual holi takes place sometime in the month of *Bhālgun*. A tree or a big branch of a tree is planted in the center of a square outside the village. The Warli does not seem to worry about the type of tree that is taken from the villagers and/or collected from the forest. The owners themselves are sometimes surprised to see their valuable piece of wood is kept as surety and with a small contribution it could be taken back by the owner.

This feast is usually celebrated by the *kārbhārī* of the village. Some people with the *kārbhārī* go to fetch a bamboo tree. The *kārbhārī* ties a string to the bamboo plant and pulls it and cuts it with a sickle. Then it is carried to the spot of the Holi celebration and kept leaning towards the main tree with a live chicken tied to it on the top and the fire is then lit by *kārbhārī*. The bamboo long is pulled out by the children and the live chicken is thrown into the blazing fire. The Warlis don't seem to be curious to know about the significance of this festival about the meaning of the rituals that are performed. This feast is a ganda feast they say. It is certainly not the feast of the Warlis but borrowed from the neighbours. The celebrations differ from village to village though the main items are the same. Normally the Warlis will not go stealing, but hold some items of the village as hostage as a part of fun.

They dance around the fire sometimes till late in the evening. The *Kārbhārī* makes some rice balls and distributes them. The following day sometime at noon the household gets together and mixes some mango flowers in rice balls and light a lamp with two bricks on for Hirva Dev and one for Naran deva...this lamp is kept on the middle pole of the house. After eating the ladoos, there is a general permission to eat raw tender mangoes henceforth. The following day dust throwing begins. *Fagawā* is demanded from house to house. Several children and women stand blocking the roads with long ropes or twigs and demand fagawā.

If someone shouts at them they will leave the rope and run for life.

The Warlis do not seem to know the traditional version of Holī. Holī mātā being burnt for her sin and the brother who shouted at her was told by the deity to take ashes and smear himself. This festival once again is taken from the larger society and is celebrated in a Warli way. They call this festival *shimgā*.

Eating of Kolī

Two weeks after the first showers in June the Warlis eat their first monsoon vegetable grown on the hills known as *kolī*. The blades of this lily with white flowers are plucked when tender and cooked very often with dal. The family members along with some elders and near relatives sit in the house. They light a lamp to the household god "Hirva" and then distribute the cooked vegetable. Liquor is also served to those who wish to drink. Warlis believe that they must eat vegetables which god in his bounty has given them after a period of twelve months. And if they don't eat it today they should, abstain from it for five years. After eating a little they all rise and meet again for supper which follows soon.

In some villages the second Gāva deva *pujā* is performed. Collection is made from the villagers. The Bhagat with some elders go to the Wāghia god at the outskirts of the village with some *kolī*, coconut, rice and a cock. An offering is made by the Bhagat, who gets *vārā* (possessed) and after eating the cooked offering (cock) gives the general permission to the villagers to begin eating the koli vegetable.

After the harvesting the fields the sheaves are brought and the floor is prepared (*khala*) (a threshing floor) with a pole at the center. A *ghad* (whiff) of paddy is kept near the pole in the center with small seven heaps of rice, around it. They are offered in the name of *Pāvsā deva* (god of the monsoon), seven in the name of durung deva, (god of the hills)...seven in the name of *samīndar...samīndar* (god of the sea) and seven in the name of *sarovar* deva (god of lakes). Similarly, another seven heaps are made of the outer ring of the *khala*. Then all these heaps are smeared with sendoor powder. Some agarbbatis are lit near the center pole. The Bhagat then takes a cock or a hen and cuts it at the top of the pole and smears the blood. A sheaf of paddy is kept on the top of the pole.

After this, threshing begins, winnowing is done of about two or three quintals and is heaped on the *khala*, the following articles are kept inside the *rāas*. Five coconuts, one stick of sugar-cane, four small bangles, one black *gathī* (necklace), one tichli plantains, dhania, white carrots, some raw onions, one piece of ginger, raw turmeric pieces. It must be remembered that these are the items which are not allowed in the Warli life, before the monsoon begins. It is after the *rāas* that such items can be consumed. The new fruits vegetables, from the house garden are kept on the *rāas*.

After sun-set the Bhagat sits at the *rāas* before the household. He invokes the Hirva deva and calls for his spirit into him (hirva *devācā vārā*). Thus he gets possessed. The house-wife performs an *ārtī* to the Bhagat then to the rāas and finally to the pole in the center. The Bhagat takes some pieces of the pumpkin (*dodkā*), *kohala* (mash pumpkin) plaintain, white radish and keeps on the *rāas* and breaks a coconut. Toddy is served on a leaf to the parents...a little poured on the *rāas* by the recipients, and then consumed. The pieces of vegetables are given in kumbha leaf to the parents. Thus they break the day long fast. They are not supposed even to wash their face or brush their teeth before they break the fast.

The cock is now cut and kept near the *rāas* and the parents prostrate to the Hirva deva, then to the Bhagat, rāas and the pole, and finally to the ox and cows. The cock is then roasted to remove the feathers. A left leg of the cock is kept aside hanging on the *palād* (hut). The Warlis choose this method of cleaning. Even the goats, pigs are cleaned this way. After making the pieces it is cooked along with pumpking, etc., and a good meal is ready. Liquor is served and all eat with joy of the harvest. The long period of semi-starvation and fasting from certain vegetables is over.

The left leg of the cock left on the roof is salted and kept hanging on the ceiling. As soon as the *malnī*, the last operation of harvest is over, it is cooked with some vegetables and eaten by the family. This *rāas* ceremony is done by all those who have land.

The *khala* now becomes a place of re-creation. Most of the Warlis begin to live on the *khala*. They make fires and warm themselves during the cold winters. It is difficult to find the Warli at home. Several friends gather together on the *khala* and often eat and drink to their heart's content.

The new paddy is heaped around the center pole with the gate to enter into the ring. The Bhagat faces the north. To his left seven heaps of rice and to his left seven heaps of rice and to the right seven. These heaps are kept in the names of 1. pānglaya devī, 2. vāvdī devī, 3. halphia samīnder, 4. sarover, 5. tawlve darung, 6. hirva (gharcha deva), 7. pavada deva. To the right mash pumpkin, sugar cane, coconut, supari, dhanis, white radish (mulle) and a lamp are kept on the paddy heap. The housewife makes the parmal (incensing) by incense or oil burning and swings the plate once to the right and once to the left. The Bhagat then lights the lamp, breaks the coconut and sprays the water on the heap of paddy. He breaks the other fruits and makes small pieces and distributes them to those present. These must be eaten raw. The farmers wife makes the āarati with rice, shendoor, four wicks burning over this gifts.

The Bhagat says, "today you are free to eat coconut, the mash pumpkin, don't curse us O Lord, don't harm us O Lord, your farmer is free from today to these gifts from which he had abstained. Friends you can eat these things from today."

The Bhagat puts the rice heaps in the names of the Gods given below and then lights two oil lamps with two wicks in each, in the first for Nāran and Himāi and the second for Kansarī and Hirvā.

1. In the name of Hirvā...
2. Vedāvat anī khodāvat
3. jināvat and vināvat
4. hornavat anī kopravat

5. phulavat anī jalavat
6. shandravat anī kukuvat
7. paghavatanī masavat
8. zoting baman
9. zoting (Broom...like made of peacock)
10. pavasa i...(God of rain)
11. chittā (spotted tiger God)
12. Himai...(God of greens)
13. Baramā deva...
14. Nāran deva...

These are placed on the top of the rice line. This ritual is done for the feasts like *kolī*, *navā*, *diwālī*, *holī* and the *hirvā devacī pujā* in the same manner.

All through the winter the Warlis work hard and thresh as per their needs. They are reminded of the debts. The land lords and money lenders visit them. They have to pay for the hire of bulls, loans taken, etc., and keep something for themselves. The women folk take their chances of bartering paddy disproportionately for fish, baskets, etc. The *khala* is exposed to the rats, fire robberies, etc. At the end of the season, the poor Warli, who is a very poor planner of the future, if he plans at all, is left with mighty little for the lean days ahead once again, the cycle of semi-starvation, loans, etc., begins. Gradually, the household moves out to work, if work is available. Towards the end of March, they wither and fall sick. Malnutrition often is the cause of many sicknesses. In several villages scabies are rampant. This is due to the dirty water in which the poor Warli is forced to bathe. There are many cases of all kinds of stomach ailments, specially dysentery, diarrohea, etc., due to lack of good drinking water. So the Warlis go on from one season to another. Years go by and they struggle often alone. They age fast and then are left aside by the young ones to live in a small hut, left there to die.

Durang Reval

Three or four days before the divali feast, a small hut of leaves (palād) is made at the out-skirts of the village, near a hill. The floor is cow dunged and two flowering plants of marigold (*makhmal*) are planted in the centre. Several elders and people gather around this hut, the Bhagat calls upon the spirit, (Dev vara) Durungacha vara... God of the hills.

Bhaarambhatral vare, sauri devācā vāre, himaice vāre
Baharam deve vāre, gadavāce vāre...

The invocation of the spirits continues :

Māndhāari vital vāre, cander surya cānd sukh vāre,
mahālaxmī vāre, vajraabai vāre, tilsai devī vāre, ambāi devī vāre,
nimbāi devī vāre, sitlāi devī vāre,
nithi devī vāre.

These are all goddesses. They continue dancing and muttering prayers and ask the goddesses for their protection from the evils. Lastly the Bhootiswara...the king of the forest (*Rān bhoot*) is placated.

The cock is cut into pieces and cooked. Some contribution is taken from the house-holders, jaggery, tea and liquor is purchased. The two bottles of liquor are for the Bhagats. The *tārpā* players begin their music and the zun (Dance under possession) begins. After this a meal is had together for which the villagers have contributed rice and cooks. The Bhagat recites the prayers over the meals. After the meals, the dancing continues, they greet each other in the Warli way and go home.

On the appointed day the householder, his wife, with the *aāratī* and the cock accompany the Bhagat to the hill for the *pujā*. At the end of the ceremonies, at the *palād*, the group goes to the house of the householder. At the door the housewife performs an *aāratī*. Some rice heaps are made on the *ukhal* (the polishing floor in the house) with shendoor powder etc. Some marigold flowers are placed in the same number at the rice heaps. The householder keeps some chitar (sign) usually one rupee hidden in the house. The Bhagats get possessed find it and take it as their fees. The householder then invites the crowd for a simple meal. Sometimes the group keeps on dancing the whole night, while others, sleep around the house like dead soldiers. The host and his wife fast on this day.

Divali

The Warli Divali is not a festival of light. It is the eating of the *cavlī* vegetable and *vāluk bhākar* (bread made with cucumber). The date of the divali depends upon the *bāras*, followed by *taurus*, *chaudas* and *punīv*. On this day, the elders from the house or a Bhagat of the same clan take the family god, remove the deities, from the basket and the basket with fresh cow dung. The deities are washed in milk or rice water, sendoor is rubbed on the gods (Hirva, Himai, Nāran, Bharan etc.) For this ceremony the Bhagat or the elder observes a strict fast. Only after the bath in the evening the gods are touched after that the fast is broken.

The housewife touches the lamp with joined hands, prostrates to the house members. She cooks *cavlī* vegetable, makes *vāluk* chappaties, and the occasion is blessed with a chicken dish.At about 12.00 a.m. the household members sit around in the house. The members of the same clan get-together and share the cavlis, chaappaties, savalia that are distributed by the elder and eaṭ. After this liquor is served and all have a meal at their own homes. Whilist eating the elder says "Midday is our divali lets eat and drink and be merry" Towards the eveing, the *tārpā* is brought out and all the young and old dressed in variety of colors dance in open. They dance the whole night often. The hills resound with the sound of the *tārpā*.

In the morning, the cow herds have their fun. All the animals are gathered together and fenced lightly keeping one side open with some sheaves of threshed paddy making the threshold.The cow herd boy brings *bhākar* and some vagetables or fish along. The Bhagat leads the cow herds with one holding a ball of cow dung, the other some food and they go round the ring. After the second round the cow herd boy with the food runs away and the Bhagat throws the cow dung on him .... then taking his sadgol makes a noise of the tārpa and shouts, the cattle are excited and are made to run to their stable with their tails in the air. There is a great joy and all run about shouting and rejoicing. A good meal and some colored clothes makes the day special for them.

Chapter 5

JĀAT : PURIFICATION RITE

Jāat is a purification rite. The Warlis believe that a person can be contamintaed (*bātlā*) if, he kills a cow or even injures it, he kills a bull or injures it, he eats from the Kathodi house or an untochable chambhar, he eats at the house of mulims, he is handcuffed by the police for some crimes, he eats or drinks water from the prison and i˜ he has a sexual relationship with a non-Warli, etc.. If a War.. woman has relation with a non-adivasi she should go and stay with him. if she returns to the village, she is kept aloof from the houshold in small hut. All food is given to her outside if she does not cook on her own. She should have her own vessels to cook or receive her food. She cannot enter the house of her parents and is not supposed to touch the utensils. *Dis* (death ceremony) is not performed on the death of a Warli woman if she had sexual relations with non-Warli. She lives inder the stigma all through her life.

The culprit is made to sit in the house and all the elders and Bhagat with other people sit along with him. The guilt is made known to all. The housewife is told to make *bhākara* (chappaties). The Bhagat makes a ghat (a circle) on the freshly cowdunged floor. The sendoor is spread with a stick and small heaps of rice is kept in the rim of the *matka* in one hand.

The Bhagat begins his chants (*Gāvlis*). Bhagat goes round the culprit seven times with a shaft in his hand and begins his chant .

Mahādeva Gangā Gouri uṭhali sakālce pāhari
asā tu māze āmce bhārajā tār mālāvar chal
āni ghosālyā bhātācā bhāt pāḍ
ukhalāvar nevoon kānḍ sadī cticaul
kanḍun de ātā ghunṭilā nevoon piṭh daloon mālā de
ātā Mahādevācā hātāt pith dilā tāmbyābhar pānī dilā

nāk tonḍ cār pāy keli; sepṭi keli; khānd kelā ḍole kelā
sāt gāyini pāvlyā
korā selā ānlā, āni ānalyā jatila gāyi hotyā sāt gāyi
koryā selyān zākun thevlyā; kāsi tarī devāci vidyā hoti
tī soḍli murud pāni gāyivar sānḍlā gāyilā
saktivāti āli gāy jivanta zālī
cālti zāli mahādevān kāthi hāti ghetli
deva hotā to gāyicā govāri zālā, gāyi cārāyā kelyā
roḍe manelā nelyā tathun vālalyā.
kasāre mānela carat ne khānogar dongarālā nevlyā
battis unḍe nele, sāt rātio sahā divas rāhalyā jangalālā,
tikaḍsi devān gāyi vālalyā dupāri bharlyā,
ṭembornichā zāḍ hotā
tiyā zāḍākhāli gāyi goṭhlyā, gāyi
mojāyā lāglā sāhi zālyā gāyilā gāyi nāhi tar
gavasāvā jato, ātāsi jāijā nakos,
gāyi gavsoon deva haṭlā
pan tyala gayī kai gavsat nāi.
devala poṭī bhook lāglī hoṭī tahān lāglī,
magā gaṅgā ātha hotī pān vāhit hoti; devāna mānḍā vāloon
pāni pilā, deva mangā tayā gangele cālāyā lāglā; tātha ūgisī
zal hoti, tyālā gāy ghutalālā hoti ti gāy meleli hoti; ticyā
mukhāsi pāni nigālā hotā
te pāni mīhī pilā
mang majyāvar ātā jāt paḍli; gāy marte khanḍālā sāvay keli
mang deva nighoon gelā gāyi hotyā tatha, tyā sahā
gāyi hākālalyā carat carat;
tyācyā ghari ghevoonn gelā; goṭhit
gāyi bāndhalyā; gāyicyā goṭhit deva baslā;
tyācī bhātāri tyālā
bolā lāgli ki gāyicyā goṭhit basū nako itha ye
to goṭhit basoon paḍla bāyi
bolāva tarī to uṭhat nāi; ātā
māzyāvar jāti paḍaliyā; gāyi maroon geli ticyā mukhāce pāni
pilyāvar jāti paḍlyā mī tyālā hāt
dharat nāhi ievan pāni mālā

vādhun dyāvā; khaoon pinoon to nighun gelā;
rāti vartoon gelyā
sakālcyā pāhari uthalā phirun thyāce bhārjālā bolu lāglā
ātā devālā bolavāyachā bharamdeva bolāvalā;
nāran deva bolāvalā
bharanbā deve bolavalā gāje,
bhirjā deva bolāyā lāgle ātā bharam deva tu uṭh mukuṭhāci
kāthi jātici kāthi ghe, tyānā
tatha ghāṭ bharlā (sendoon soḍun)
chavlāchyā puralyā thevlyā tyāvar bāriksā maḍkā ānlā
tyāt pāni ṭhevlā ticyāvar korā sela ghātlā;
tyācyavar devālā
hāt thevāyā sāngalā; bharam deva muṭhāchi kāṭhi ghevoon
uṭhalā devālā bolāy lāglā;
atā devān pāni pilāy āhā jāt padli āhā yāchi gāvli
bolāychi āhā tumi deva ho āikun ghyā;
deva bolat āhā hātāmadhi
kāṭhi hoti ek bhāl hoti;
pāni uḍvat hotā chāri bajulā tatha deva
gāḍhi bolat hotā...sad gāvṭhi sadāchi asi vāvadhī bhānoji bīs
sat pheke deva phirlā hotā sat gāvṭhi
satāci āsā bolat hotā bolat hotā bhis
atā panch lokā ho devaci jāt zāli gitā tumhi bolā
zāli dhvanā tasā bolā
devāne pāni pilā
tyāci jāt zāli
atā māji cuklā tar asā jāt pāthāvī
ātā se gāvṭhi bolāvī jāte karoon ghyāvī. (See app. 5.1)

(Summary Tr.: The Mahādeva gangā gaurī got up early in the morning. " You my beloved go and bring down the "Ghosal paddy" and pound it in the ukhal to make some clean grains, and take them to the grinding stone, and make fine flour and give it to me." I gave the white flour in the hand of the Mahādeva and poured water upon it. The Mahādeva mixed the atta and made balls, then he formed them into shapes of cows. He made seven cows, with mouth, noses four legs etc.. and these seven cows become propitious.

The cows are taken to the pasture land of the Rokohde and from thence grazing went to the Kasara pasture lands and from there to the hill of Khangone. He took thiry two flour balls and stayed for seven nights and six days in the jungles. Then the Lord took the cows to another lands. It was the height of noon, and the cows were hurdled under the shade of tree. The lord then counted the cows and found only six cows. He spoke to the cows "I am going in search of the lost one. You keep safe here, don't stray yourself." The lord was tried of seacrching the missing cow but he could not find the prodigal. The lord was hungry, he was thirsty and his lips were parched. He came across the Gaṅgā, and the Lord knelt down and drank from the flowing waters. He roses on his feet and walked along the bank of the river. Suddenly his eyes fell on the Ukshi creeper mesh and beheld a cow who was entangled in it, and closer he found that she was dead. "I drank that water, the highest sprits saw it and I was defiled." He thought.

The cow was left in the valley of death, the lord of the spirits went back to his herd under the tree. He drew the cows grazing along and took him to his abode. He tied them in his stable and sat sorrowful. His wife requested him to leave the stable but he sat with his head in his hands "I am defiled". One had died and I drank the fluid from her mouth and I will not touch anything you serve me for food. After having eaten and drunk from her hand, he slept. The night rolled by he rose up early in the morning, and once again he called the Lord Naran, call the Lod Baramba, and all the thunder lourds were called. The whole house was filled with gods and they spoke. "Rise take your scepter and the staff of your race" There he smeared the sendoor and kept the thiny heaps of rice in their honour, a small pot was kept over it with water and covered with white cloth (shaw l) and ask the sinner to hold the rim of the pot.

The seven images are covered with a white piece of cloth. Thus the wishes of the goddess are fulfilled. Holy water is sprinkled on the cows and a lif was breathed into them and they began to ealk. Mahādeva took his staff in his hand and became a "*Govārī*" (a cow boy) of the cows and he led to the green pastures. This "gāvli" is repeated as the Bhagats takes his seven holy rounds over the penitent who has defiled himself by drinking outside his caste.

The lord took the septre and stood and began to invoke the chant, "Now the sinner (god) has drunk the water and has defiled. I have to sing the gāvli chant, you gods listen to me. He held the shaft in his hand and the spear in the other and sprinkled the water in all the directions and there the lord was chanting gāvli "Sāt gāvri sadci asi gāvli". Now ye the elders of the village, the sinner (god) has been purified and now you may speak, if purified say so, if not withhold the pardon. Henceforth if and man sins let me be purified in like-maner, sing the same chant and wash your sins.

The Gāvlī continues further, the pentitent smears the shendoor, cuts a cock and upon the god of the sea, he lifts the pot and puts water on the hands of the penitent. If he is purified, let it be so. Then some water is poured on the floor. The penitent makes a cone with a leaf and washes the toes of the Bhagat and the elders and the sips from cone. He calls upon the gods to bear witness and the Bhagat says "If you are clean drink of this cup. You drank the forbidden water (from the hands of an outcast), and made yourself unclean but now your sin is forgiven."

The Bhagat says to the penitent, go in peace and cook the cock of your offering". He then calls for the rice chappattis and cooked meat and gives it to those present ..." Today you are made clean let no man accuse you of the same guilt lest he be condemned. The penitent pays a fine according to the offense and gives some money to the Bhagat. He takes the bread and meat and liquor and offers it to the panch and people saying "If my jāt is regained eat and drink from my hands otherwise refuse it and throw it to the ground."

The penitential rite is done for all the sins committed by them as mentioned above. And this sin must be mentioned while reciting the gavlis.

Chapter 6

JOLI-LAGIN-DIS : THE LIFE CYCLE RITUALS

Joli

"ais vaharal tar dhavoon jai jos".

"If mother calls go running to her". It appears that the father can teach wrong things to children while the mother is the true companion of the child. After the above line is chanted, the child is lifted from the cradle and is passed under the cradle to the mother thrice, and then kept in the cradle again. The *suini* takes an axe if the child is a boy, and a sickle if a girl, and passes the same way round the baby. The child is then taken out and handed over to the mother. In the evening some elders and near relatives are invited for a simple meal of rice and curry. When the child begins to walk, some months, the nurse is given some money.

Several children get an attack of tettanus. The main cause is the *borru* stip which is used to cut the naval cord. The nurses do not take the care to wash their hands with a soap or with any disinfectant. Some experienced *suinis* (nurses) seem to know a lot about the position of the baby in the womb and often help the young mother for a safe delivery. Most of the Warli mothers are very young and have difficulties at the time of delivery. Several first babies are pre-maturely born due to mal-nutrition etc. In general delivery cases among the Warlis do not create many problems. Their regular hard work and exercises help them a lot.

From the time of birth till the end of *Jolī* ceremony the *Saṭhī* is observed. There should be no roasting of fish or meat, no giving of fire coals from the house to the neighbour. After the *joli* ceremony dry fish bombīl (Bombay duck) is roasted and served to the mother. With this the *Saṭhī* restrictions are over.

Before the baby is put in the *jolī* a string is tied to baby's neck, hands, feet and the waist. Some rice is put with money in the *joli*. It is a ceremony of the intiation of the baby into the community. Though the ceremony is done by the women folk, there is no restrictions on any men being present. The only reason for having the *joli* rite within three or four days is to make the mothers free to take part in the household and other work.

Passing the baby through the Umber Tree

When a baby is sick with rickets or is showing signs of thinning, the parents accompanied by a Bhagat go to a nearby umbar tree and make a hallow through the tree or use the one, that already exists. The parents stand on either side of the tree and pass the sick baby once or twice as the Bhagat suggests. This thinning sickness is called *ravdi*. A feather of the ravdi Ṣ(a bird that is seen rarely in the jungle resembling the bat) is tied on the neck hands and the feet. The Bhagat chants the following prayer "Oh god, this is suffering from the birth of rivad sickness, please stand by and cure him. Forgive his sins and evil he may have in him." The Bhils also use this method when a child is sick. They pass the baby through a kin (kin in Warli is a tree hole).

Lagīn

The parents usually choose the girl. They approach the girl's parents and make the proposal. If the party consents then they immediately drink liquor. A promise is made. After this the following ceremonies take place.

Badhāvani

Two elders with the parents go to the girl's house and pay Rs. 5/- to the village panch. There they drink and settle the details of the marriage transactions.

Dez

The *dez* is taken on the shoulders by the parents of the boy to the girl's house. At the girl's house the door is locked by two *savasinis*, with two *musals* (threshing bars). These *musals* are decorated with mango leaves and umbar leaves. The four bearers carry the paddy and one *paili* of tur on the shoulders to the door. The luggage is smeared with sendoor twice.

The *savasini* at the door asks 'what have you brought?' *Ṣrani ghanö* reply the bearers. ṢFrom where does this come ?ö *Ṣghata barsiö* (from the hills), reply the bearers. The *savasini* then strikes the parcels four times with the *musal*, once in the front and twice from behind. Then the *savasini* makes the aārti by taking the sendoor, rice with Rs. 2.25 and seven vicks in it. Then she makes the *aārti*, puts in a *tilla* and prostrates at the bearers feet. Then the bearers enter the house saying, *rām rām* to the elders who are sitting in the house. The parcels are then emptied on the *ukhal* in the center of the house. These parcels contain eight brinjals, eight errandi fruits, eight turmeric pods, eight val paddy, two in each parcel. Now before the elders Rs. 21/- are kept in the *aārti* plate to feed the near relatives of the girl. Rs. 65/- are given to the elders to divide it as follows : Four bottles of liquor to drink together, Rs. 20/- to be given to the parents. Rs. 1/- to the khatia (village intermediary between government and people appointed by revenue department with a small salary), Rs. 2/- for the patil of the village, Rs. 1/- each to the two *savasini*, Rs. 0.75p for the *varghoda*, Rs. 1/- for *karbhari* and the balance is distributed among the elders. (The amount have now increased manifold.)

After this the boy's party returns home, drink and eat along with the group that had accompanied the *dez*. The *varādhkyā* (master of ceremonies) is appointed at the girl's place whose duty is to master the ceremony. This, requires approval of the panch who accept two bottles of drink and approves the master of the ceremony. The master of the ceremony fixes the date for the purchase of wedding clothes and other requirements. On the date fixed, two *savasinis* and four people from the girl's side and the parents of the boy with hishousehold members enjoy a special meal at the boys place and then proceed to the market. The saris are chosen by both the parents, one red, one green and one white sari. They also choose one pāsodā for the boy, A *pagadi*, a long shirt, one *dhoti*, one *sala* (shawl) and two *polka* (blouses for the girl).

The relatives of the family also get clothes which are bought at the same time. The things which are bought for the relatives are : one sari for the girl's grand mother, one for the mother, one white cloth for girl's brother, one choli for the sister, choli and sari for each boy's sisters and one *dhoti* each for the boy's brothers, one pāsodā is also purchased for the master of the ceremony (*varadhkya*) and *dhaklis* and *fuis* get one sari each, though of a cheaper quality. They also purchase *Perranni (aher)* of twelve dry bombils for the patil, kadkdi. Tumbdi, sarees, *basinga* - (two) each for the boy and two for the girl. Four *gathia*, 8 bangles, one *gal soot*, eight *suparis*, two *phani* (combs) sendoor, five coconuts, tobacco leaves are also purchased along with one *bhal* and *supari* to be carried by the boy.

Wedding Ceremony

This ceremony is performed five days after all the purchases have been made. On the first day a *mandap* at boy's place is painted by experienced ladies on the wall of the house in the main room. Usually, rice flour is used for this purpose. The figures represents the king and the queen. Prints are done by dipping the side of the closed fist in the mixture of the flour and the water. The main theme is the king and the queen on the horse, and some sepoys at their side. They manifest the husband and the wife as the king and queen of the house. During the pendol construction, gram and jaggery are given to the workers. Sometimes drink is also served.

The following day, the girl's *mandap* is made by the girl's parents. The poles are of ain tree, sixteen for the boy's *mandap* and nine for the girl's *mandap*. At the center of the *mandap* one *umber med* and at the foot a basket with *musal* (pounding rod) with rice husk, two branches of the umber plant, two clean sticks of umber are kept. One *savasini* and one man with a cloth piece on his shoulder and the other end on the elbow of the *savasini* and some umber branches in her hand go round the center pole seven times and leave the leaves in the basket below. Another one with a lot of water with a mango leaves and coconut on it goes before the pair carrying umber, as she goes, she sprays water.

The bridegroom is made to sit at the side of this basket in the center facing east. Then two men, preferable the pātīl or kārbhāri (having land) do the bāsinga mode on the chowk of the house. They both hold the bāsinga on the chowk and sprinkle rice grains on it twice, then, facing the sun with *bāsinga* in the hand, spray rice twice. They come to the pendol in the center repeating the same process. Eight of the household members are made to sit around the bridegroom and the bāsinga mode is done the same way by the two men.

Now it is the turn of the *savasini* to perform the same rite. After this they return the bāsinga to the two men who tie it on the hand of the bridegroom. The *dhoti* is tied, the shirt is put on, the pagdī is placed on the head, with the *pāsodā* flung over the shoulders and finally the selā is tied on the head.

While the bridegroom sits in the center, turmeric powder is mixed in little oil by the *savasini*. The bridegroom stands and dips his little finger in the mixture and applies it to the parents first, then to the brothers and sisters and the pairs sitting along with him. After this, it is applied to the panch mambers. Finally, the *savasini* applies it to the bridegroom.

The same ceremony is simutaneously repeated at the girl's place also If the toddy is served baachka is put in the pot. If jaggery is served it is put in the winnowing fan.

After this the drinking session begins. The head of the *panch* (*patil* or *kārbhārī*) takes a drink in the leaf and spills it on the floor and says, ŞNow give one helping to all present, if it is not sufficient, provide, even if the collection is not enoughö. If toddy is served all must be served. After the drinks all sit and have a simple meal. As soon as the meals are over the bride-groom is taken to the bride's place.

Padāva

This ceremony relates to the camping of the boy's party at girl's place. The boys party is kept in a house near the girl's. Then the *pātil* or *kārbhārī* of the place invites the party to the girl's house. They are given two liquor bottles, the bridegroom is lifted and then taken to the bride's place. At the door step, two *savāsinīs* greet him holding two *musals* (pounding rods) across the door. The girl's brother stands behind her and say :

Ṣbhutālkī lāgal, sinālki lāgal tar
tujī novrī pasant iāli honī tar tit hāt
ghāa nāhītar tujā kharchā mofat zāyil.

(Tr. : ṢWhether she is possessed or has fallen in impurity, you have chosen her to be your bride, if you have not, your expenses will go wasteö.)

The Bhagat puts some coins in the plate, with rice, sendoor and Rs. 1.25 for the *savasini*. The bridegroom is now taken to the center of the room and made to sit with the bride on the *ukhal*. The bridegroom takes the gāthī (mangal) sutra from the kārbhārī, while facing the east. The brother of the bride stands behind and says Ṣchinch pad, chinchan jalava, amba padal ambiana jalava, yakhada tar taichi kasti tula dhuyaciö.

[Tr. : If tamarind is dropped, hold it ; if mangoes are dropped, hold them for her ; if she is sick take care of her and wash her linen] Then he turns to the girl and says : Ṣsukh dukh zala tar kasti kargota tula dhuvaichaö (Tr. : ṢIf your husband is sad or happy, wash his loin cord and cloth. For better or for worse accept

The marriage pendal is made a day before the wedding ceremony. At the girl's place the pandal consists of nine poles, while at the boy's place it has sixteen poles. The reason for this difference is not known. The poles are brought to the site of the pandal by two persons. They stand facing the house and a *savāsinī* makes an *āartī* to the poles held by two persons. Then the pandal is erected in the morning of the actual wedding day at about eight a.m. A lady and a married male go to the outskirts of the village and bring some branches of the umber tree. They are accompanied by a *savāsinī*, *turā* (band), *dhavleri* and *karāvalī*. At the foot of the umber tree a small place is cow dunged in the form of a circle and smeared with some turmeric powder and rice flour, and two *vainā* (small rice chapatis) cooked in boiling water and placed on it.

Surya Modini

One pounding rod, a basket, some paddy husk are kept at the center pole of the pandal. Though the meaning seems obvious, no satisfactory explanation is available from the Warlis. Two gents bring the *sada* about (three saris tied in bundle in a cloth bag) and face the sun with a little rice grains in hand and sprinkle it in the four directions, twice at each direction. Then to the *umber* and to the *kunbis* (a farmer with some prestige). The *savāsinī* repeats the same to the *kārbhāri* who is sitting on the pandal. It appears that it stands for the horns of the deer, the kingly animal of the jungle. this ceremony which is done in the morning is called *surya modini*.

Deva Chowk

This ceremony is held in the night. At the boy's place, three *dhāke* Bhagat (those who play the *dhāk*, a musical instrument), one zun Bhagat gather at the night. Two of them get possessed by the spirit sit facing the wall where the *chowk* is made. The *chowk* is a square design with some typical Warli theme done with rice flour and sendoor. Another *chowk* is made on the floor just below the chowk on the wall. This is popularly known as Hirvā deva *pujā* among the warlis. The following morning the *savāsinī* and *karāvlī* go to the village well and bring some water and leave it in the pendol. After this begins the *dhan moznī*.

The *savāsinī* starts making small circles from the kitchen center of the house, at the entrance inside, one at the main door entrance and one at the centre of the pendal. Every ring has a heap of rice. Then the bridegroom comes to the kitchen in his ordinary clothes, and is made to sit on the mat (pidda). Two *savāsinīs* hold a winnowingn fan above the bridegroom's head containing a waist chain, some rice, *bāsiṅgā* and dry *ambādī* stock. The brother of the bridegroom is next to him with a cloth piece round his head and the *ambādī* stock in his hand. Holding the chain in both his hands the brother makes some signs in a form of a cross in the winnowing fan and leaves it in another empty winnowing fan. This is done four times at every circle while the bridegroom is carried with his bride for the ceremony till the center of the pandal.

Bath

The bridegroom is made to sit in the pandal and the *savāsinī* takes a pot of water and sprinkle the bridegroom with the help of a mango leaf while they pour water on the bridegroom. He gets up three or four times after a good scrub with soap and the *savāsinī* carries the bridegroom on his pat into the bouse. The bridegroom dries himself and puts on clothes.

Invitation

The two accompanied by an elder go to the village and invite the people for the bāshingā ceremony. The elders gather in the house. The bridegroom is dressed in his wedding best and sits on the lap of his father in front of the wedding chowk. The mother sits beside. The *kārbhārī* or *pātīl* conduct the *bāshiṅgā* ceremony while five pairs of the village elders sit close to the pendol.

Bāsiṅgā

The *savāsinīs* come and put turmeric powder on the bridegroom's face, hands and feet. Then they mix some with oil and put it on the fore head with some rice stuck to it. Those sitting with the bride groom also get the share of the turmeric powder. Meanwhile the *kārbhārī* pierces the *bāshiṅgā* to tie the cords. Then he asks the people and the elders seeking permission to tie the *bāsiṅgā*, saving "does anybody have any objection if I undertake this ceremony". The people say "no". Then *kārbhārī* and one of the elders both hold the *bāsiṅgā* with both hands and make the *ovālanī* twice on each shoulder. At this time an exhortation is given by the *kārbhārī* to the bridegroom : "Today we have gathered together and after undergoing a lot of expenses have organized this ceremony, loans have been taken, so don't forget your parents respect the elders, and don't run away from your responsibility. Work hard and try to repay the loans". Then the *bāshiṅgā* is tied to the forehead of the bridegroom. The silence is broken and there is singing by the *dhavlerī* who sits at the side with the wedding lamp along with some women. This lamp has small suparis tied to it to show the members of the wedding ceremonies conducted by the *dhavlerīs* (priestess). For a Warli wedding the *dhavlerī* is very important. Then *turā* is played and there is rejoicing. The people are invited to bring their *āher* (gifts) for the bridegroom. Then those who make these gifts are given drinks according to the amount given.

Rām Rām Ceremony

It is the last official ceremony of the wedding. The bride and the bridegroom are bathed and dressed and made to sit in the pandal facing the East. The village *Kārbhārī*, the panch members (elders) sit around. The *varādhkyā* sits behind the bridegroom. One respected person from the village sits behind the bride, the *kārbhārī* normally appoints him. The person who sits behind the bridegroom makes the *JOHĀR* :

vātā ghātā saarkār darbār
lātā totha, patel tāṅdel
savāsnī ture dhavlariā
samas mandalī...johār...
re johār...

(Tr. : O givers and takers, elders and youngers, *patel* and tāṅdel, *savasini* and priestess and respected guests, we welcome you.)

The *kārbhārī* takes some toddy or liquor in a earthen pot and asks someone in the gathering to make a hole in the pot by using the spear knife that, is in the hands of the bridegroom (*bhālī*). The toddy is given in the palms of those who sit around. Then once again the *johār* is said and little toddy is poured on the floor. Then the leaves are distributed (palas leaves) for a large share toddy is served from the pot after the words vat...ghat...as above. Then at the end *rām*...ram is said by raising the leaf cup a little...all say *rām*...*rām*...and drink in honour of the new couple.

The *savāsinīs* come with a plate of turmeric powder mixed with water and apply it generously to the bride and the bridegroom. Beginning with the shoulders, knees, ankles and finally on the back. The bride and bridegroom give some coins to the best man, *varādkyā*, and prostrate at his feet. They or the parent keep some coins in the plate of the *savāsnī* and light the *pantī*...(lamps) in the plate.

Vātvā

The crowd from the pandal with the bride and the bridegroom go outside for the vatva. Here a cock is cut by the *Ture* (band players) and is roasted on fire to remove the feathers and is prepared on the spot, small places are distributed to those present. Toddy is served to a few or tea. The bridegroom goes on wishing all in a traditional Warli way...(holding the elbows and swinging them a little). The bride touches the feet of those present and all disperse the bride goes later to her mother's place.

Motha Mul

Five days after marriage the bridegroom accompanied by a people go to the house of the bride, where some people get-together in the pendal. The sut thread in the neck is made and the bridegroom ties it around the neck of the bride saying...

māji kāni tujā galā
kazaa kāmālā jāin
ta hariz vi jos

(Ts. : My ears and your neck, when you go for work, we will always go together.)

Then the bride ties the *kargottā* (loin string) to the husband. (This string is made from the string that was put round the neck of the bride and bridegroom on the wedding day...). The string is put around both the bride and the bridegroom. After this ceremony, the bride and the bridegroom with the *kārbhārīs* return to the bridegroom's house. After two days the bride is taken to her house by the *varādkyā* and near relatives.

Bārikmul

This is performed after five days of the marriage ceremony. The bridegroom goes to the girls place where good lunch is made and household members eat together. By evening the new couple return to the bridegroom house.

Adjustments at the New Home

Often the new wife finds it difficult to adjust herself to the new surroundings. Sometimes she tries to escape from difficult situation and goes to the parents place. The in-laws try to bring her back and try to make her understand her responsibilities. Sometimes she never gets used to the new home. So another marriage is planned and the *dāvā* is paid by the new would-be husband.

tī zāin tailā rāhāli
māhāti padlī; dēvā maṅglā; dāvā bharlā; bāiko sutli...

(Tr. : She went and stayed with him, it was known. The compensation was demanded and it was paid. Then she was free.)

Pregnancy

Most of the Warli women give birth in Divali or in the months of June or July in this area. Soon after the arrival of the new baby the umbilical cord is cut.

The umbilical cord is buried to the north side of the house along the house walls. The baby is bathed by the point by the *savāsinī* in hot water and then the mother. After two days the child is cotterized with the help of a hot needle to stop vomiting. The mother is often massaged on the stomach and is fed by rice *cunji* for two weeks. She is not allowed to touch vessels and remains under certain restrictions.

The eldest person in the house does not touch that baby for fifteen days. Any women suffering from abnormal menstruations. (*dokyāvarchā ye*) and others who complain frequently of abnormal bledding. (*raktī mahal*), also and not allowed to touch the baby.

Pandal

The pandal consists of poles from the forest. In the girl's place the pandol consists of nine poles, referring to the nine months of gestation. The boy's place has 16 poles, referring to the age of puberty and adulthood. In the centre they put a pole made out of umbar tree. Two baskets and a pounding rod (musal) is placed at the root of the central umbar pole.

First Bath

The first bath is given to the new couple who sit on a *pida* (a wooden flat stool) of the Warli... Some oil and flour is put on their backs with turmeric powder on the back and a big matka of water is poured on their head then they are carried by the *savāsinī* on the stool to the house. This first bath is a test bath, if any signs of sickness or unwanted pregnancy irethere.
A typical form of drawing on the wall is made by the *savāsinī* or some special artists of the village. This drawing is done out of rice flour. The sketch resembles a throne. It is consecrated by a religious ceremony conducted by three Bhagats.

Second Bath

This bath is in the pandal before the audience. This is for the verification of defects once again. After this the couple get the consent from the public to go ahead for a happy married life.

Ottani

The bridegroom is taken on the shoulders outside the pandal with dancing and playing the band and then made to sit on the floor outside the compound of the house. Here the *bāsiṅga* of the bridegroom is changed and put under a piece of cloth. Then it is taken rejoicingly to the girl who sits near the chawk. The bāsiṅga of the girl is taken and put in a similar way to the bridegroom. Then again the process is repeated and the bāsiṅga returned...Then the bridegroom is brought to the pendol on the shoulders and just before entering the pendol the *varghodā* takes place.

Warghodā

Some people hold a bamboo stick across the bridegroom and make some demands. They usually demand liquor or cash. After the demands are met the bamboo is broken and the bridegroom is allowed to go. The parents and near relatives following the bridegroom are annointed with the turmeric on the forehead.

The bride and the bridegroom are made to sit around the *ukhal* with some men around the girl and the boy. A heap of paddy is put on the *ukhal*. At a given signal, both the parties grab. The one who grabs more is clever.

Vidas of Mango Leaves

The *savāsinī* keeps the rui flowers on hands, shoulders and head of the bride and ask the girl to pick them up. On the hands, mouth, shoulders and feet the bride picks it up. This ceremony is repeated three times. The same is performed by the bridegroom too.

The *bāsiṅgā* of the girl is removed by the little finger of the boy. The hair is removed in the same way thrice. The boy does this while sitting, but when the girl does it she stands. Then they proceed to the maindoor of the house.

The younger brother is made to sit at the main pillar at the house with an axe on his shoulder. The couple asks him "what do you want from us?" The boy answers, "wife". The couple answer, "we will provide." The couple give the young lad some coins, the boy gets up and strikes the med with the axe thrice. The mark indicates that while this sign stands try to get me a wife and the med stands for a witness. The bridegroom lifts the bride and she ties the *bāsiṅga* to the *med*, thus the *med* becomes a remembrance and witness to the marriage ceremony. The couple is made to stand outside the main door and the young sister sits with the caravali pot on the head behind the door. The couple ask to open the door, the girl refuses. What do you want from us...? husband answers the sister., Then she opens the door. Some coins are given to her. The coconut is broken and is shared by all present there.

The couple proceeds to the pandal and sits under the umbarmed with some rice and coins. Some near relatives put turmeric and the couple put some coins in the plate. Some toddy is put in two small pots and is offered to the people around.

Ukhardi Valkarni

The bride carries a basket of cow dung from the stable to the *ukhardi*. The *gal-sut* is hidden and the bridegroom blind-folded takes it out with his feet. This is done three times. The bride wears the *gal-sut* and comes to the pandal.

The couple sits around the *ukhal* in the room, with four more couples with rice chappatties and chicken. They eat and then go to the river with soiled clothes along with the *varādkyā*, to take bath and drink.

Johār

This is a sign of salutation to the elders. The Warlis raise one hand and other hand touches the elbow by the saying ram ram. This is done only by those who are married. Others not married do not have the right to do so.

Parnai

Making a hole in the pot by the *phāl* which the bridegroom carries all along the ceremony as sign of a conqueror...marriage by conquest. A right to use the marriage and rights over the wife.

Dis

As soon as a death occurs in a village, there is loud mourning and weeping. The whole village soon knows about it. The Bhagat of the place is informed. The elders get together and are told the cause of death. The distant relations are informed. As they approach the house, loud cries are heard. The body is covered with a sheet and left on the floor. Two pots one big and one small are purchased from the potter. Rice is cooked in the small pot and water is boiled in the bigger one to bathe the dead. The dead body is made to stand and is bathed with the help of the pumpkin spoon (*dāvli*). Water is poured four times with the help of the *dāvli*. The near relations then give a bath as a last good deed.

Some seeds of the erandi fruit (seven of them) are woven into a stick and burnt under the blunt edge of the sickle till thick smoke is formed. A white clothe is spread on the ground and the corpse is laid on it. The loin string around the waist is removed and a new one made from the ambadi plant is put instead. A new white loin-cloth is put on. A pagadī is put on the head, the soot from the sickle is removed and put on the eyelids. Sendoor is applied to the forehead, two dots, on the shoulder, two dots on the hips, two on the knees and two on the toes. Similarly, the soot from the sickle is applied. The cooked rice is then tied in cloth and kept on the chest of the dead as food for the last journey. The small pot is filled with burnt cow dung and kept in the sling. One of the elders carries the burning pot and a winnowing fan with some rice in it and lead the funeral procession. The body is lifted on the shoulders of four people as they proceed to the cremato-rium. The corpse is taken seven times around a bush near the crematorium. The big earthen pot, the pumpkin dāvli and a mat which was immediately used is left at this spot. The pyre is laid and the corpse is kept upon it, it is fed with the rice that is left on the chest by four people (near relatives)...

Pahillā khāsi ghāsī...ātā vasī khāi jos...

(Tr. : In the beginning you ate, now you smell and be satisfied.)

Some liquor and water is poured in the mouth Rs. 1/- is also put in the mouth. One each in either hands, 25 p. on the hip and 20 paise on the feet, that the dead may cross the seven gates (sat chaukyas) towards eternity. More wood is piled and the pyre is lit by going round the corpse.

One of the elders in the family lights the pyre, the mourners remain till the ash is separated from the coals. The ground is swept and cow dung is lit.

The party goes to the nearest river, bathes and returns home to take some liquor. If some charred bones are left they are taken a little distance and buried. The group chants...

pahilā khasī ghāsī...
āta vasī khāi jos...

(Tr. : when you were alive you ate the normal way. Now be con-tent with the smell.)

The last smoke on the cremation ground is the final sign to hospitality. The women are not allowed to the cremation except the wife of the dead, who remains present there to break the *mangal sutra* (*gathī*). The finger of the dead man is put on the *gathī* and is broken. If the dead person is a woman, then the husband breaks the *gāthī*. The ashes are not usually put in the river but only washed off. If the river is nearby then some might put the ashed in it.

Those who die in epidemics like cholera, small-pox, leprosy or women who have lost their issues pre-maturely for several years or if there is no living issue, are buried with their faces down-ward, with a hope that their sickness will not return the same way. Pregnant women are sometimes buried and sometimes cremated. Specially, when the foetus is not removed, the deceased is buried. All women dying with a pregnancy have their dead foetus removed by a crude operation with a sharp knife by the Bhagat. The foetus is buried far off. The stomach cavity is filled with cooked rice, so as to make stitching operation easy.

The Warlis believe in life after death, and they placate the dead so that they would not disturb their community. There is no positive interest in the soul of the dead. Once the *dis* ceremony is over, everything with the dead is over. Hence, the Warli is very particular about the *dis* ceremony. He will not celebrate any wedding etc., without finishing of the *dis*. Once the soul of the dead descends in the pot kept in the small pandal on the day of the *dis*, it is believed that the soul now is in peace and happy. Death means separation from community and this will be established by the *dis* ceremony. Physical death does not mean much to the Warli.

The hot water for bath must not be mixed with cold, since it will be impure. While the procession starts, from the house some grains are thrown in front. After the burning some rice balls and cavli is left in the place of cremation. The Bhagat does not look at it while placing it, lest the spirits get frightened. When the people come home after having a wash from the river, the Bhagat says :

jivālā mara nāhī, parmaswar dātā anī tochanetā...

(Tr. : The soul is not dead, God gives and God takes).

The body of the dead is kept facing the North. No one knows the reason. May be that since the Warli descended from the north, his feet are facing the north and his head is to the south. Meaning, he began his journey from the north and ends it in the south. In the ceremony of the dead the names of the main gods are not mentioned.

māmze lādkyā bahve yare yare
māji pāth kon rākkhil re bhāvā
mānze bhāve yānā yānā...
tule kot nāgo re bhāve.

(Tr. : Come back my dear brother, who shall look after me, come back my dear brother, where can I find you.)

Dis Ceremony

This ceremony is for the dead. The Warli is restless until he has finished his duty. Only after this he can go ahead with other family feasts with joy.

The date must be fixed by the party concerned and the Bhagat must be informed accordingly. Six small earthen pots, six coconuts, one black *ghati* with a white *khadī* (ring) two small bundles of thread, four plantains, four betel leaves, four dry dates (*khari*), four *supārīs*, sendoor, one white cloth (loin cloth size) and twelve dry bombils, are gathered.

The Bhagat with three assistant Bhagats sit near the pandal and ask for the "vattva" i.e. a bottle of liquor. He then takes the *māli* leaves and makes seven garlands and keeps them hanging under the ceiling of the pandal. The var (small earthen pot) with water is taken and the garlands are dipped into it and a coconut is placed on the top. The Bhagat orders the household head to distribute drinks (liquor, toddy) or tea to those present as the party can afford. After this a simple meal of rice and dal is served. The share of the dead person (food and drinks) is put on the "*Karvali* leaf" and placed on the pandal. As the food is being served, to others two people carry the food of the dead with both hands and leave it besides the fence saying : "We have kept the food for you, please come and eat it..." Of course the dead does not eat it. After this rite, all those present begin their meal. The Bhagat pours his drink to the mother earth and prays to cānd, surya, suk surya, abhasaar deva, jogeswar, mangeswar, ganngeswar, vijeswar deva...etc...and brings the gods to earth chanting : "Help me lord that I may utter the words without fail and forgive my sins and clean my heart". Thus, begins the long chanting of the Khands. The earth Gods are invoked by reciting the Khands or chants, such as

1. The Namni (abortion chant).
2. Kiran chant.
3. Kulvadi chant.
4. pan ungle dugia chant.
5. Parni chant (sowing of all kinds of seeds).

Here the Dharti chant is sung and after this follows the Mohala khand, the Somin khand, Divla khand and the Hirva khand. While the chant is going on people throw coins, rice on the floor before the pendol.

The full Dharti Khand is given here with a translation. The language is kept intact as far as possible for the better understanding and the original version is also attached.

The Dharti Khand

eke ṭāṭicā ho jewālā basā.
par jāti havā te uṭhun bājulā whā,
āj āmhālā mansuā tyāci jāt karāyci āhā.
kāsichā bāman ālā āhā to jevāyāsāṭhi bolalā āhā.
ātā saglelā hukum dilhā jevā ātā.

pārvati tu gharā rahejos
tāhanecā yel tilhā pāni dijos
bhukheca telhā khānā
āmhi jāt āhā dunyā nāgāyā.

sagalā wadū lāgalā, dhartilā bāhār lāglā,

gāyicā gohrā tākun lāglā, kombḍā vayā karayā lāglā,
gāyicā gorhān ṭāpri mārli ta ājagi dhartarī phoḍun lāglā,
asā bhār malā nāi samā vat, jāy ātā mi maran karāyā.
māhādeva dādāsi jāy maran karāyā.
raḍat zaḍat jāt hoti raḍat geli dārāsi.
vanasā dādā koṭha gelā āhā;
dādās gele dunyā nāgāyā, gangā gaurīsī.
tu kāy raḍas?
tahān lāgli havi ta pānī din.
bhukh lāgli hovi ta khānā din.
pan dādās nāi ta māghāri walīv.
māghāri walun phirun raḍat jāt hotī.
tatha gāyica goṭhani hotyā,
tatha hotā hisāv pānḍku bhukū pānḍu,
arjun pānḍu, hote.
tyacyā gāyi goṭhavilyā hotyā.
titha vidā hāti hotā.
tisī khelnā khelat.
dharti raḍat zurat geli hotī.
phuye tu koṭh jāte hoti?
vi geli hoti dādāsi.
dādā ghari mila nāi.
kyā geli hotis?
ta maran karāyā, gelī hotī, jātā vetā karāyā geli hoti.
phuye rāngaye na malhā sāng.
baharā āhā, malā kānāt aiku yet nāi,
rāngaca geli bolāyd lāgli
mī jātā yetā maran karāyā gelī hotī.
tyālā rāg ālā, hātālā dharalā phiravle nā zokun dilhī.
gol kankārē zugarun dilhī
tath raḍat hotī,
tikadsi mahādeva gaṅgā gaurī walali hoti dunyā phirūn.
gaṅgā gaurī mahādevālā bolāyā lāgli,
gol kankāri konitari zurat āhā.
āpan nangāyā jāv.
nāgāvalā tar dhartibāi āhā,

tulā dharti kāy zālā?
sukh hovā ta dukh tuzā, nā dukh hovā ta sukh karu.
mālā kām āhā, mālā jātā yetā maran karāya āhā
mālā nāy samāwet
hātālā dharalā nā uṭhavli.
tuje māhāli calatulā jātā yeta maran āmhi
maran karun din.
tatha gaṅgā gelyāvar devā geli.
mag icswar devāne māhalā bharli.
khanḍun khandācā viḍā sivlā.
rājun rājāca, khanḍun khanḍācā.
yek viḍā āhā to maranācā sivlā,
saglā viḍā parātit ṭhevle,
devālā hākā mārlvā,
deva rāngun gele.
rājā hoti ti devān ghetli.
khanḍun khanḍā ghetli
rājā ghevun (jyāca tyāca rājā ghetāli) deva gapp rahale.
yek vidā rahatāi yek rāj rahalāy wātāycā.
wāṭun tumhālā suṭi din asā dev bolat hotā.
pānḍu deva hotā. tyācā hotyā don bhātāryā.
pānḍu deva sakāli uṭhun pārdhilā jāt hotā,
dupāri bharlyā na parat ālyā.
tyācyā doghi bhrataryā bolāyā lāglyā.
devān māhalā bhavli, rajvat
deun devāci rajā ghetlā,
mang pānḍu deva bolāyā lāglā.
yekhād rāj tari mihu ghein
ieswar mahālālā gelā, pānḍu deva.
maranācā viḍā hota to,
payāce bhovare mārun ujavā hāt tāklā.
to viḍā uchalalā hotā maranācā,
ardhe wātelā jāun nā phoḍun nāgjos,
sāre devāna (hoti tavḍelā) suṭi dilhi.
deva nighun gele.
ardhe wāṭela pāndu deva gela,

vidā phoḍun lāglā.
tyāt hoti marnāci chiṭṭi,
vichar karāyā lāglā ke āpun viḍā uchalalā pan bes nāi,
maranācā viḍā āhā.
ātā yālā kāy karāvā.
tyālā ḍokā dukhāy lāglā.
tuje devā bahanis āhā ta kāv vicār karāl.
maran nāy karālā.
pānḍu devā vicār karit hotā,
tyācyā hotyā doghi bhārajā,
doghi bhārajā lāgalyā bolāyālā,
āhā devā tumaci bahanisā,
kāhitari vichār karajā.
pānḍu deva ta gela nighun,
rāhat karit hotā,
bāndh bāndosti karit hotā,
lāglā bāndo jeṭhācā māhanā,
yāci kāmā lāgali cātāyālā
tyāci hoti satti kahamari
tyahce hote sathi nāngar
yāde maradā. nāgar hindavat hote
hi tyāci kāmar (kāmawālī)
bhāt khanat hoti
arpanāce kām tar cālalā hota
bhātāryā ta khanat re hotyā
ātā mardā āvāyā geli
ātā devā āvāyā ra geli
na sāthī nāgarā hinḍavat ra hote
ciravarā pānā karat re hote
teeth mardā āvatā re hotya
bhātārya āvatā re hotyā
pānḍu devāt gelā nighun
bhātāryālā suṭi dilī re hotī
nāgarelā re suṭi dīlī hotī
tatha āle bailāce govāri
manga deva lāglā bolāvalā

tilā mardā lāglā bolāyalā
govāri ho tumi jāyajā gharā
āj ta mi bailāsi rahalā
pānḍu deva ta bailāsi rahalā
bailā walat hinḍa
hotā pun to gāyicā gorhā
pānḍu devān kasā nāngalā
pānḍu deva ta gelā nighun
gāyicā gorhisi gelā nighun
gāyicā gorā kyā re hasalā?
pānḍu deva ta gelā phasun
himā devisi pāy yāce āhā
tuze devā maranā tilā
himā hi pāyta kasā suṭal
tujā pan to jivḍā neti
gāyicyā goryān to akal sāngto
meḍe māhali jayjo nighun
tuje māhali jāyjo nighun
bes meḍi tu bāndhjo
yek kholi māwali ṭhevjo.
sāt kholyā tu ṭhevjo
yek kholi māwali ṭhevjo
sātihi kholyā changlyā ṭhevjo
tatha tu to hadupā ṭhevjo
haḍu pyālā pāthi ṭhevjo
tuje ghar ti gosā ānjo
tuje mahāli gosā ānjo
komboḍice māsā anjo
tatha surā tu ānjo
dāru ānun taiyār ṭhevjo
loṭyā sheḍci ghāgri ānjo
ghāgryā ānun dorilā bāndhajo
mājhe deva pāyilā bāndhjos
tuca mardā tayār rahajo
mica te sāngun pāhajo
ghāgryā mangā sānjun pāhajo

hāti tu dhvanaṭ ghijo
malā tuje sangāti jevādhajo
khursi dun dewāl dijo
devā tu ātā bhās jo
dongrā jāyi kāy dekhāy
gāyicā gohrā nācun paḍlā
khurshyā dādun devālā dilhyā
dādā ho tumi atā bhāsā jā
jumā shivāy kursi bhāsle
devāce dekhat padalyā
pānḍu devā dekhat pāḍalā
ṭoḍlyā pānḍu lāglā bolāyā
tinā surā ānlāy
pahilā surā tina analyā
bhakaricyā bhājyā ānalyā
kombodichā bhājyā ānalyā
mangāyinā dārvā ānalyā
mangāyinā dārvā ānalyā
pānḍu deve to phār cānglā
jumā sipāi māgā zumlā.
cal devā kholyā nāngāyā
tujā kholyā cal nāngāyā
nighun gele movle kholyālā
pandu deva re lāglā bolāyālā
ajun kholyā gele re nighun
nighun nā gele hadpyāce vāle
jummā sipaī hāḍāpe halava re
hich kholi phār chāngli
pahali hoti tilā pāhun
jummā sipāi ṭākli konḍun
jummā pāy haḍpi konḍun (See app. 6.1)

(Tr. : Listen oh people, lets eat from the same plate, those from outside our community please keep away. Today, we want to placate the dead. The brahmin from Kasi is here. He invites us to the meal. Now I invite you to partake of the meal come and eat now.

The universe was filled with all kinds of creations and it laboured under its weight, a young bull bucked the earth and the cock scooped the Dharti with its feet, another bull dug the earth with its horns. Dharti cannot bear such a burden.

She goes weeping to the house of her brother, Mahādeva and asks her sister-in-law Pārvatī : "where is my brother Mahadeva?" She replies "Your brother has gone with his wife (ganga-gauri) to see the world (Dharti). If you are thirsty I will give you water, if you hungry, I will give you food. Since the brother was not there, she returned weeping, towards the cow stables, where she met Hirav, Pandu, Bhisav pandu, Bhikoo Pamdu. Arjun Pandu and veir. Cattle were tied in the stables.

There was a wild elephant also and they were busy taming it. They saw Dharti sobbing and weeping and asked : "Aunty! where did you go?" I went to see my brother Mahadeva. "Why did you go?" "I went for the funeral rite", (Dis) she replied, "to liberate the soul". "Oh Aunty come near and tell me I am deaf, I cannot hear, she came near and spoke "I went for the liberation ceremony". He (Pandu) was angry, he caught her by the hand and flung her into the gol kankara (gol kankara dunia) the whole round world. There she wept, and Mahadeva and gaṅgā-gaurī saw her while returning from their world tour. Ganga-gauri said to Mahadeva, I hear someone sobbing bitterly in the gol kankar (earth) lets go and see", They found Dharti weeping. "What's the matter Dharti? If you are happy we will bring sadness, if you are sad, wew will bring happiness (meaning we are capable of doing anything)". But Dharti replied—"I have work, I must perform the ceremony of liberation till then I am restless".

Mahadeva took her by the band and said : "lets go to your palace, we shall perform the ceremony". The great God Iswar invited all the corners of the universe and kingdoms, and prepared the vidas (strangular folded leaf) one of the vidas represented death. All the Gods invited came. Each God took the kingdoms quietly.

One vida (lot) was left and with it one kingdom. After this choice all gods were told to go. But Pandu Lord was missing, he had gone for a hunt in the morning leaving his two wives behind.

By noon, he returned and his wives told him that the great God swar had collected all the gods and filled his mansions and distributed kingdoms by lots and every God has taken his share. The Lord Pandu, said to himself "I will go and take one of the kingdoms of my lot". He entered the palace. Only the death vida was left, the Lord Pandu swift on his feet, grabbed the lot of death. He was told by Ishwar : "you shall go half way and open your lot". The assembly was dismissed and the gods had returned. Lord Pandu had reached half-way and he opened his lot. To his surprise it contained the chit of death. In a pensive mood, he said to himself "I have chosen the lot but not a good one. It is a death chit. What shall I do"?

His head reeled and he prayed thus "Oh God! my wives are your sisters and I know you will be considerate. You will not kill me".

Pandu was in a deep thought. His two wives began saying, "Oh God! we are your sisters, be propitious to us." Then Pandu went to his fields to do his work.

It was the month of May (summer time). He was busy with his servant who ploughed his fields. The woman dug out the seedlings and the transplantation was over. The married man and women transplanted and the gods too joined them, they ploughted and puddled but the Lord Pandu left his fields and gave a break to the women and the plough man. The cow boys were told to leave the cattle and keep them with him (Pandu) while he grazed the cattle, he saw the male one amongst them that mocked at him and Lord Pandu saw this and went to the bull and questioned, "why did you mock at me". One of the gods intervened and said to the Ghora (bull), "Do you know that he has the Himai deva (the whole nature) under his feet. You will die and Hima (nature) will not spare you. He will take you life". This same god inspired Pandu also to go to his own palace and build a good house and, "have seven rooms, keep one extra room empty. Furnish all the seven rooms and the one that is empty will be fixed with a strap that opens one way. Then bring chicken meat, toddy and liquor and keep everything ready in your place. Get some trinkles from

Lotia Seth (bori) and lace them in a string and tie them around my ankles."

"Think of me and join me. Give a chair to the Lord and request him to sit. The cow fell from the hill before his eyes and the bull began to dance. The lords were given the chairs. "Friends be seated here" the Jama sepoys (death mourners) and the Gods watched and the Lord Pandu spoke. They brought toddy, and goat meat, chicken meat and liquor and the lord Pandu also brought his share. He is a good God and the Jama sepoys began zun danic (dance under possession of spirits).

Come O Lord and see our rooms. They passed through the rooms and came to the empty one which had a trap laid in it. They found the room better than the other rooms. There the god Mahadeva locked the Jama sepoys and the Lord Pandu escape through the trap door.

The Lord Pandu was the first to die because he choose the chit of death and paid the penalty for his absence from the day of distribution of the kingdoms. Some Lords choose the moon, and became Candra Lord, Some chose thunder world and became thunder Lords. Some choose hills and they became the Durung Lords etc...but Pandu chose death under deception and became cursed and had to die.

His two wives approached Mahadeva and obtained the way of a escape for Pandu. The Lord Pandu stayed in the sea. His food was served to him by his wife and his son. One day his son found a bora (berry) on the tree. The child went to his mother and showed it. The mother out of compassion for the father asked the son to give it to his father, Pandu. The son offered it to the father. The Jam sepoys escaped from the captivity and hide in the berry in the form of a worm. The Lord Pandu ate the bora and die.)

Thus the Lord Pandu fell under the curse of death. The whole universe mourns his death. But Dharti to Mahadeva saving that where there is a corpse there should not be sorrow. Others must smile and be happy. Thus the Lord Mahadeva orders to perform the Dis ceremony. So for the Warlis, Pandu's death was the first death of the universe. The Dis ceremony, thus is performed by the order of the great God Mahadeva. This ceremony teaches the Warlis the inevitability of death in the earth and tries to bring back happiness and joy to their otherwise hard life.

After all the khands have been chanted, the main Bhagat (zun Bhagat) sits near the pendal cuts a cock and breaks a coconut and commands the "pitar". An assistant Bhagat sits near him beside the pendal to take rice into his hand. The spirit enters into him. He breaks the garland and the ghati (black necklace) from the pendal and holding it on his hands runs about the crowd, blowing his hands and searching for the immediate friends of the dead for a hidden article (one bottle of liquor and some coins). If he finds it he takes it for himself if not the members of the household keep it. Often with the help of some known persons or children the pitar finds it. Some believe that under the spell of the spirit of the dead these articles are located. Senior Bhagats seem to have the power to locate hidden articles.

The pitar goes to the pendal and takes water from the hands of the people. This water is taken from the pot kept in the pandal. The Bhagat then rises and says ;

> "daya maya azshi andich anzashi rada bada bund;
> azshi yachi athavan nai karaichi; ata visraicha"

(Tr. : With this our love and compassion is over. We should stop mourning and weeping. We should not remember the dead, we should try to forget).

Pitar

Pitar is a small Bhagat who is chosen to take part in the ceremony of the Dis. He joins the senior Bhagats at the end of the chanting all through the night before the pendal. He slowly gets possessed those present sprinkle him with water. He then gets up breaks the garland in the small pendal and holds it tightly in his hands. The household people holding the lotā in which there water and give the pitar to drink. This lotā is held by all the members of the household. The pitar drinks it. Then he gets up and runs throwing coins at the people, meets the mourners and wishes those intimately connected with the dead person. He searches the hidden article which is the main proof that the soul of the dead which is placated is saved, if he fails then the household gets nervous and approaches the Bhagats who then tell the party concerned that an additional sacrifice will have to be offered at latter date.

The pitar after his short journey to the nearby houses returns and sits near the pandal. The sympathizers band through the pandal, throwing small coins and rice on the other side. After this the pendal is demolished and thrown into the nearby river.

APPENDICES

APPENDIX-1.1

भूत पिस दूस्मन दगा आहे कायबात
देवाची दगा आहे
नये बालकाची
बंदोबस्त करून दे
आनी खाता पानी पिता करून दे
यो तुइयावर भार आहे
चदर–सुर्याचा किरण मोकला
तर हया बालाला मोकला कर, मुकला झाली पाहिजे
पांच दिवसाची बायनी धरत आहा

1.2

हे देवा ही विगना आली
तापी विगना, आगी विगना,
अडया दावना खरज्या दावना,
दवना, मुरडया दावना,
चावही दावना,
ही विगना आली आहा आपल्या गावात
गावच्या देवा, तु पाठीसी उभा रहजोस
काना आयकून, पन दोली खाल नाय नागू
तर तुला खरी मानू,
खाली येती, वरून घालवजोस
वरून येती तर खालून धालवजोस
असा देव पाठीसी उभा रहजोस
नारलाचा फल, जामिन ठेवत आहा,
सेंदराचे डबे, दुपाइचे परमल,
असा गावात विघना, आला नाय पायजे

ते दूर करजोस, ही पुंजा तुला चढती होईल,
चारी खंडा जामिन, दोनी जगा जामिन,
आठ कोट राजा जामिन, नव कोट खंडा जामिन,
ये खंडाचे देवा, जामिन नवसाला उभा रहजोस,
रांडे–मुडेचा नवस, पोरा बालाचा नवस,
ढोरा–ढारांचा नवस,
सेती वाडीचा नवस, मोठा नवस आहे
हया नवसाला उभा रहजोस,
पाय कड नाय आला पायजे, सिरेकडे नाय आला पाहीजे
सितलय, देवी, गाव सितल, ठेवजोस,
पानी प्रमान सितल, दूधा प्रमान सितल, ठेवजोस,
हीवसे समंदिर, हिमा पाडजोस
तेय समींदर दिना पाडजोस

1.3

सकालच्या पाहरी सूर्य तो उगवता आहे
यानी त किरना सोडली आहे
मुलात समंदिर किरनात उजेडला
चारी ते खडात किरनाती उजेडली
गायीची ति भीरडी त सुटली आहा
आहा ती ताना पडा गायीची
चरायला लागली आहा
वरली ती कुंदा ती त्याची ती चारायला लागली आहे
तसाच तं निघून गेला आहे
तसाच ते सिंदाचे बुडासी गेला तो
वनसीचे झाडावर उजवा हात टाकला आहे
पाला तो तोडला आहे, चोलात तो मलात तो
रस काडला आहे तसातो सरपानने
मिरीथा मांजीनी सरपथ ते दुसला आहे

1.4

नाथा गुरु आदम नांग सुखा सोडू सोडाविका
पासाना बालू येरे विका, कोठो होतास, डसलास तो
तुझी विका, तुझी लाहरा सिपली काठी पहिला फूल
गानी वानी विद्या धेतली हरावंती, येरे विका
कुठे आहे सुतीती, वालला आहे
अरे सापा होतास कोठ, तुझी कांनची
कानच मार आराप डेबरून, सर्दीचे तयची तयकानची होता,
तयत आराफ डेबरून फोऱसानच्या कनची होता
अरे विका वाला आहे
तुझे विका तुझी लाहरे पान्या शारख्या,
ठेवली नाहा, दुधा सारखी सिताल झाली, नितल झाली
मिरया मिर गुरकि, टाबोलकी, सिसार की पाहराबादू
गोपी भगत मरे सांगाया गया कास्पा दूसल्या
जानवर निगोरे विगोरे

✯ ✯ ✯ ✯

APPENDIX-2.1

सकालच्या पाहार तो लागला आहे
चंदर, सुर्य
चांदया याना किरना सोडली आहे
समींदर उजेडत तसा तो कायाल
महामती महादेव वरत गंगा–गौरी
उखलत, मुसलन, खावरंग
घेतली आहा, सोनीते मालवरी चढली आहे
कोन्पा पाडल्या आहात
खांद्याना सडका तांदुल केले आहा
तसे ती अधेरी खोलीला गेली आहा, कंगाल तो टोफ

★ ★ ★ ★

तसी
चोलली, घोवली, घानली
अग्ने बल लावला आहे, पानी तावला
वजरा सिलापानी नेला आहे, ठेवला आहे
महादेवा हाका मारली आहा, आंघोली कराया लागला आहे
दातवनी घेतली आहा, जिवईचा चानफल
धरतीवर टाकली आहे त्याच्या गांडूलात जमला
लोहटे मार्गीला चालला
चंदर, सुर्य किरनात सोडली आहा
गांडूलीच्या मरना झाली
तसा गाडूलया धरतीच्या पाठीत गेला आहे
धरतीचा करनार झाला आहे
भातात, गंगात, गौरी ही तयार केली आहे
महादेवा हाका मारती आहे
जेवताना जिववा हात घुवले आहे
गुरूल तसा तो उठता आहे
मोयटीच्या काज्या घेतले आहे
सोन्याच्या जल घेतले आहे

बरात बेनती तथ देवाला हाका मारली आहा
तसा महादेवान बोलवला, देवाच्या पारोडी बेसली आहा
तसा झाला त फोडून दिला
भावाचे विगनाचे जत गिर मुलाचे चल फोडून तू दिजास
तसी ती बिघना धरून बांधून दिजा
रखवालाचे मेरी काठी (मांजी)
जिहीर हुना ताप कादून धिजा हिवसान वारा
चंदर–सुर्य जगता चांद जगता झाला आहे
सुकेसर जगत झाला आहे
जगेस वर जगत झाला आहे
विजेसर जगत झाला आहे
गढेसर जगता झाला आहे
माझा झाला तो फोडून दिजा
खैरेसवर जगता भोयेसर जगता
या जात देव जगत गोरी जन देव जगत
नकेसर देव जगत झाला आहे
तसेच विघना धरून–बांधून दिजा
बाल धरतीवर पडला आहे
धरून–बांधून देव हो दिजा
आता काजे, दावे हाताचे भानसी
गुरूचा मान, फुलाला भार झाला आहे
चंदर सुखाचा किरन, मोकला करजो
तसा बाल हिडता करजो
उन्हा तो ताप कादून धिजा दे
वावढी वारा वरसेत
राझाला रमत, बरम देव वरचे राजाला आहे
मादेरी देव तो
तथ हुमाय देव, वरचे राज्याला देवा केला आहे
हलकेत जगतात केला आहे
मोठे समींदार ओलांडे जगता
ही सेन गोरान–बिया, संदीरता हिम बसाया

हिसम समदीर तसा जगता केला आहे
तडहेत समदीर सितल्या समदीर
सितल सिवाल्या समदीर
सितल–नितल करून समीदरो
हातोबा देव सावरन, करत आहे
पतसेड चार पथून पाच उभा रहजो
सफरचे वेलीत करजा, रजीत
पोवेतला सात से उपटे रहजा
वेघाटे नडगासी झोबीत नाको सावजा
वाघाच्या धोंडीत करजा गुरूच्या पाठीसी ३ भारहजा
जिवादानी जगती माहादेवाचा दीवला जपता
तसा वावटीचा चेडा जगत
माकरीत चेडा जगता झाला आहे
हुबाचे झाड जगता
टिपरीबा देव जगता झाला आहे
सुनाट मांडव जगता झाला आहे
सोनिचा दरवाजा सिव जगता झाला आहे
महा लक्ष्मी जगती झाली आहे
वजराकाय, तुलसाबाई जगतात
कलकादेवी जगत्यात विगना धरून बांधून दिजां
अमबय जगत्यात
निमयन्देवी, सितलय देवी जगत्यात
माझा नितल्य देव रामताय देवी जगत्यात
मसायदेवी जगत्यात झाल्या आहा तसा जान ते बरहोनडे
सहराला
येत पाढला आहे तथ गावचा देव जगता झाला आहे
तसातो गावचा देव जगता
आपल्या गावाला विडना आली आहे
धरून–बांधून दिजा गुरुचा मान करात
गाय गवरी पढली आहे
खीनटी

कुथनी हिन्टीन हानयास गायीचे
चरायला लावजास
जगली चेडा महारीत जगत
देवा हो करत आहे
माझा जल, भूताचे विधना नावाचा झाला
कोरेट घाटात आहे
फोडून दिजा गोधानोनेला चेडा जगता झाला आहे
गारदी चेडा झाला आहे
सकाल पाहरा लागला आहे
तसा चंदर तो सूर्या उगून आला आहे
किरना सोडली आहेत
मुल समीदर किरना उजेडला
तसी गंगा गौरी निघून गेली
तसी सावरंग सुपात घेतली आहात
सोनीत मालावरती (माची) चडली आहे
तसी कनसरे पाडली आहा
खादाना काटली आहा
कनी कोनडा वायला केला आहे
पहला गंगा गौरीचा निवाडा लागला
तस्या चोलल्या नयी राम नाय वीघना
निघां आता, काय करावा?
तरी पन दादा नको भी जो
फिरुन बत्तीस उसील (डोंगर)
चनेच्या झाडसी गेला आहे
उभा रहला आहे, चनेच्या बुडावर चढाया लागला आहे
उनवत—नाव्रत मरत आहे,
नाय पानी—पाऊस मिल,
तसा देवानी खंड, तसा नादाला मरत नाही
पानी पाडास मिलत
लक्षीमन देव कसा वसा दिसी झाला आहे
मंगा राख नाद्रात तरी पान पानी
पाऊस नाय ती मिल

तस्या मावतसी नादारत मारल्या चऱ्याचे
झाडा वरसी निला बाल संगती
वीच्या सारोवार पानी नांगला आहे,
चऱ्याचे धरतीवर ठेवला आहे
मुठ अडकल्या गावात सोडल्या आहा
सरोवरी जात उभा रहता आहे
मुठी अडकल्या कलंगडी निड केल्या आहे
पानी त बुडवाया नेली आहा
बालातीन सावरीचे हाका मारले आहा
दादा नकी पान्याला हात लावजोस माझा पानी दे
हिरवा गार थंड आहे
बुडासी गेला आहे,
उजीत पान तोडले आहा
कोल्हा वाला आहे
पानी घेतला आहे
मुठी ओडकल्या दावा दे बारा बेलोटनी आले आहे
वाटेचा खंडा चुर भुका झाला आहे
निघून चाललाय केलीचे खांबासी केली
फिरुन पडली आहा
वसी मिरीक माज्याची दुःखा मुठांचे
चावलाचे भाराखाल मुठी वालून दिजात
तसा रामा लक्ष्मन देव आला आहे
रामाचे जायाला आले आहे
वनसाया खुडल्या आहा
चोलल्या रस वनसायाचा काढला आहे
रामाला इस्वर देवाचा ना बरमदेव निवडा दे
सती जिवडा सत्येचा लिहीन
तगदीर खरा लीहेल हवा
मुठीचे खांडेखाल तसी गुरुचे
शब्दाखाल उतरत
खाली नाम उतरसी चावली सुर्याचा किरण मोकला आहे
तस्या त्या मुठी लागून गेल्या आहा

तस्या बाराला चावरा (चावटी) सोडला आहे
आग झाली आहे
गुरुचे देवजी गुरा भिमा गुरा घाली गुराचा मुठ वालून
दिजो
गुरुचे सल्याखाल नाय वालसी
वुला प्रिया (अब) तसी मला नाही प्रिया लागला
चावस्या मुठी झाल्या मुठी चकल्या मुठी चावलस मुठ
या मुठी गुरुचे शब्दाखाल निकाल
गुरु बाबा त्या जाते तानपर जाते
वन जलवे गुरुबाबा तपान कर
बोधना कर तस्या मुठी घालून देसील नाय?
वालसी माझे गुरु घालसी मगारे वालसी
डावे पायाची लाथ मारुन तसी मुठ वालून देऊ
आभालात चांद बसला आहे
धरतीला पथार बसला आहे
वसा बालाचा बान बसला
समधी निरमल झाला आहे
पलखाखंड गरजाय गंगा गौरी निघून गेली आहे
काम कराव तापले गायीचे सीतात
टोपली आली आहे
सकालचे पाहराला उदले आहे
तसी कसारा मानीला सिना गवसाया लागली आहे
तसी बारुथ मानीला गेली आहे
तसी सिनात नाय मिलत आहे
पाठीसी उभा रहजास रातीला सात फेन्या
दुखासी उभा रह जिनीतबाई तीच्या कारनी निघून
आवा कुहलाबाल गायीचे पोटासी निघाला
चांगल्या त्या चांबज्या कोनाया लागला आहे
चादर एकदा देव पाठसीला उभा
करनीबाई बरनीबाई तोटलीबाई भिडलीबाइ स्वेचा
दुखाचा

सदबंध किहून जाती हो
बनसे कोनाचे नावी मरत आहे
दु:खाचे नावी तसी निधून चालल्या
धरतीच्या कोहरन्या झाल्या आहा
तस्या त्या दु:खाच्या कोहया करत आहे
गुराचे शब्दाखाल देवाचे नाव मीठी करम खोरा
कराल अरे पुन देवानी अक्कलनांगला घेता
तसा अज ते चालाया लागला आहा
आती काही दिजास माजेचे प्रमेसर देवाचे पाय
हात, डोले, तोंड, बोलाया चालया दिधील आहा
वसा हिंडता करून तसी दु:खा मारून गेली आहा
तसी सोहरनी चालया लागली आहे
चांद सुर्याच्या कोहरन्या झाली आहा
मी त्याच्यात दु:खाचे कोहरणे (काम करणे) करीत आहा
तसा सुकेश्वर देव त्याच्या कोहरनीया
तसी निघून थरसाव दु:खात झीजत नाय
कोंमबत नाय भुकत फीटत नाय
येला काय कराव निघून लागला आहे
माहादेव गंगा गौरी चालाये लागली आहे
वरात बेलोती गेली (दोघा) गेली आहा
तसा सोन्याच्या दारी देवाला हाका मारल्या आहा
देव जमा झाले आहा (लागला आहे)
देवा तू बाजूला बसजोस तो बाजूला बसला
पावश्या देव बोलाया लागला आहे
तसा यो मालात जातीचे बाहेर बसवला आहे
कुहल्या गायी धवस
तसायो जातीचे कायरे पुन मला जातीचे बाहेर बसवला
मग देवाचा तुम्हाला आता रागाचे
देवाकड जायाया लागला आहे

✯ ✯ ✯ ✯

रोहनीचा पानी पडायला लागला आहे
तरी बिया ऊंगून आली आहा
तसा दुधीचा ताना (वेल) फुटला आहे
चार मेडीचा लोहारे मंगा गरजये गेली आहे
कुरहाड कोयती करवने निघून गेली आहे
गेली गढ मलाला सानचे पाहराला
तेनी जेवना केली आहा
जिवली, भाजली, निजली गुठली आहे
सकालचे पाहराला खानगराच्या डोंगराला
वेलूत वासे तोडाया लागला आहा
दाडे बांधाला आहा उचलला डोकीवर घेतला आहा
चालाये लागली आहे माडीत माहला झाली आहे
सातचे पाहराला मांडव केला आहे
तसा दुधी मांडवावर चडला आहे
फुलून अशा गलाफुल निरफल
एकुच दुधी लागला आहे
तसा दुधी वाढला आहे
पिकाया जोग झाला आहे
दुधीची पोटात पालेचे खंड निघाला
करने भरने रांदे तसी केली आहे

☆ ☆ ☆ ☆

सहज पोटात माजीचे पोटात पहली जी आग झाली आहे
तसी दुःखा वाढाया दाने पहल लागली आहे
आता विचार घरीसी आई–बाप करायाला
ही काय दुःखा झाली आहा
करनीयाचे कारनी चालली आहे
ती बी तसा पालेचा खंड चालाया
तुमचे देवाची करनी बिया वरूनी
बिया कोहरनीया माइयाजी
पहारचे देवा कुटलबाला
माइयाच करतेचा, भरनेचा कोहुन टाकजात
देवाचा पाय दिधेत ना

तसा नाभूता (भिउ) नकों नाकोस
बिहजोस पालेचा खंड चालत आहे
तसी हाताची पाहानची दुःखा करनी बिया भरनी बिया
तोडली बिया मोडली बिया आज पाहटेसी उठून
जायजोस
हर मोजाला देव आहास
गरजाचा कुहलेबाला
सहजी पाहनीचे शब्दा खाल
ताकत वनगान वहत आहा
ताकदीची आयी जेवना रानधून दे
दादा देव बोलाया लागला
समीदर काडीत कापत जात बसला आहे
समदीर हुन समीदर सोसून समदीर घातला आहा
गाय बारा वर्सा झाली आहा
जागेलाच गाईचा तांड खपून
देव तागाडे लोलाया लागले आहा
मरून जात लागला आहा
तेवढयात इचारात तसी दुःखा
मान्याचे (पायाचे) पाहाटचे
रूजून फिटून सुखवानी खंड
रोहडे मानीला गेली आहे
गायीच्या सेतात गवसाया लागली आहे
हिवाले मानीला गेली आहे
तसी सेता नाय मीलत आहा
मुरूम मातीला गेली आहे
तरी पन सेवा नाय मिलत
मगा तांबड मालाला गेली आहे
गायीची सेना मीलली आहे
तरी बहनची पाटी भरली आहे
हाताचे जोराखाल माथ्यावर
मडी माहलीत आली आहे
सगची पाहराला रोहनीचा पानी

पडायला लागला आहे
तोडल्या सात खानीत खनला आहे
तेथ सिन तयार ठेवल्या आहा
खानगर डोंगराला गेली आहे
विरखनचा पाला घेतला आहे
माडी माहलेला आले आहे
सकालचे पाहराला उठली आहे
लागून रातखंडा दिला आहा
रोहीनीचा पानी पडाया लागला आहे
अथ मला येत पाजला आहे
तसीच तुला माहादेव बोलाया लागला आहे
तुला त्याची कडव्या कारेलाची बिया पायजेत आहे
आमच्याकडे बिया, कारलेच्या बिया नाही मिलत
मला निघून गेली आहे पाथीन राज्याला गेली
बिया मागाया लागली आहे
तिकातीज्या बिया कडवे दुधीची बिया
पाथरी (उदारी) बोलाये लागले आहे
आमच्याकडे दुधीच्या बिया नाही आहा
तसी गुगेरी राज्याला गजरांय गेली आहे
तसी गुंगेरी आमच्याकड घोसालाच्या बियानाही आहा
तसी बाय कुलण्यान्या दारासी गौरी गेली आहे
तुमाला काय पाहज मला
वयीच्या बिया सात बिया घेतल्या आहा
सात खानीला लावली आहा

☆ ☆ ☆ ☆

APPENDIX-3.1

सकालचे पाहरीन तसी तीकुलबीन निघून
पारस्याच्या दारान गेली आहा
अर दादा तु आम्हाला जाबुडीच्या होला
नागाया गेली आहा
मागून नावेटा (बंधोबस्त नाही) दिसत
कुम्बूडनीची सेती पसंत कराया लागला आहां
दोघा कुलबी विचार करत आहां
पाहुन होल्या पसत झाली आहा–पारस्याच्या दारी गेली आहां
पारस्याच्या नावावर जमीनी करून दिल्या आहां
मारी त्या माहलाला गेली
सानचे पाहराला जेवन
दोघा कुलबीचे जेवता आहा
जेवून विचार करत आहा
तसे आपूनला काय पायजे हवा
सात सेत कमारी कुलबीन लागला आहा
सजान शहराला पारसी दादा
इकड कमारी नाय मिलत आहा
तसीच बोरडी शहराला कुलबी वाडोल्याचे दारी गेली
आहा
विचाराया लागला दादा कोठे जायचा?
मला कमारी सातसेत सेती पोसाया पायजेत
इकड कमारी होती वी धाना लावाया केली लावाया
निघून गेली आहा नाहीसी कुमारी मिलत
तसा कुलबी चालाया लागला आहे
निघून पालघर सहराला गेला आहे

☆ ☆ ☆ ☆

तथ कमारी वानीचे दारासी
इकड कमारी होती पन स्वताचे कारखानी भावली आहा
नाहीसी कमारी मिलत कुलबी कसाबिसा झाला आहे
माघारी वलला आहे चालाया लागला आहे

जन्मात राजा गेला आहे पांगर आईचा जन्म झाला आहे
उपजेत उपियो राजा गेला आहे
दासाचा उबजत झाला आहे
त्वरीत कमारी नाही मील रूयी गावात गेला आहे
रूयात पुजून ते आली आहा तस्या कुलब्याच्या वाडीत
फुलून ना तसी पालसेत गावी
गुरा चराया गेली आहा
तथ कमारी नाय मिलत सी
गावचे गुरा चारी गेली आहा सिरी गावात गेली आहा
सिरी गावात तो गेला आहे
सिरी जासी फुलून तं बारा वाडी फुलल्याच्या योजो
अथ तपारी गावाला गेला आहे
सातसे कामारी तयार लि
तसी टोपरीला भिरड भराया लागली आहे
सकालच्या पाहराला डोकीवर बिराड गेतली आहा
निघून लोका (मार्गाला) चालाया
वरचे राजासी देवाया लागली आहा
गावडी वरच्या हालपेड संदीर डेवाय (लागले आहा)
जवारी सराल होती वानेरी पोटी नि भूकेली
तलपाटी सहराला सातसे कमारी डेवाय लागली आहा
पेटी शहराला लहानी फास्याला येऊन शहराला सातसे
कमारी
कुलबी मुहरापार चालत
तसी पेरोटी सहराला तेथून लोहारेत मार्गाला
चोरगाव सहराला आले आहा
तसी कोजबाड सहराला आली आहा
मनोर गावात कुलब्याचे दारासी भिराडा डेपारनी
कमारी ला तसी बसाया सांगला आहे
तसा आमली जेवता सातसे कमारीला तयार केली आहा
जेवली–बोलली (सावकासे) आहा
आथा सानचेचे पाहराला बिजली गुटली
तसा यो कुलबी सकलचे बोलाया लागला आहे

कोयती कुराडा मला रोकडा दाम दे
लोहाराचे दारी गेला आहे
लोहार कोयता–कुराडा पाजवून दिजोस
त्याचे कामाचा रचजेत आहे
वाली अशा वारली डोंगराला गेली आद्य हिंडाया लागली आहा
वराला नाय पसंत सांगाया सागवन उगलून गेली आहे
कोन्या कोडवाली उगडून गेली आहे
इनाचा इनवाली उमडून गेला आहे
मुसल दुर्गाला गेली आहा
वारन नाय मानत सूई
हिंनगडवाले दुर्गाला वारल चितामानी नाय ए तसी
मोहरले दुर्गाला गेली आहा नाय वारल नागाया
लागला आहा
कोडीचा कीडावल भारील आहे
पार वराल डगरोच्री झाए भारेल
सांगाचा झाडा वडाला भारेल आहे
माली माहलाला चालाया, तथ कीनाचा कोन होता
तिन हाक दिला आहे
तसी लोटीचे दारासी नारलाचे फला दिजोस
सिद्राचे दिजोस टिकेची, बांगडीची पुजा त
माडीत माहलाला आली कुलब्याच्या अंधेर खीरीला
गेली आहा
सातशे कमारीला बोलावा लागली आहा
पंधरा दिसाचा सिंदा वास करजास वारल तोज्या
जायाचा
रासी डोंगराला गेली आहे, सिद्राची नारलाची पूजा केली
आहे
वारली कोंबडीची पुजा केली आहे
वराल तोडाया लागली आहा
कावले वर कावती पाढाये लागती आहा
एक दिस तोडाया, दोन दिस तोडाया,
तिन दिस चार दिस पांच दिस

पधरा दिस, पन तोडून वारल पुरी केली
निघून लोटी मार्गाला देवाय लागली आहा
माडीत माहलाला आद्य
सनचे पाहराला निजाया लागली आहा
सकालचे चंदर–सुर्या किरना सोडली आहा
सातसे कमारीला हाका मारल्या आहा
निघून आल्या आहा तरी पारया पावती घेतली आहा
जामबोटीच्या डोलाला गेली आहा
ओलात बांधाया लागली आहा
नागय्या ओल्हा दिसत होतीया
सजवले आद्य फार भारीया
आता तसी कुल्बोडे ओल्हांला
बांध बांदी कराया लागले आहा
सानचेची पाहराला जेठाचा महना उगवला
रोहनीच्या उगवत री ढगदेव ढगात
गाजेसर गजराया लागला आहे
तसा यो कुलबी निघून उगवटसी नादर टाक
सातसे कमारीला धका चला ही कमारे घे, वावरत
भराय जाव
नारल भराया लागली आहा सात फाटा सातराव भराये
लागले आहा
भरून रिकामी पडली आहा विझेडी माइया त्या पडल्या
आहा
तसा राफ भराया लागल्या आहा
तसा राब आग लागला आहे
राब पेरला
रोहनीचा पानी पडाया लागला आहे
सोनेटा मालावटी, फुलवटी (घरवाली) चडजोस
बिया हरेकुडाची, जवारीची, चावलीची तुरीची
आमबाडीची, नागलीची, वालेची, बिया नाहीसी मीलत
पारसीचे बिया नागाया गेली आहे नाय बिया मिलत
मागत पहारी राज्याला गेली आहे

पातरी बियाला बोलाये गेली आहा
आमचेकड बिया नाय मिलत
आमा पाय पत्राची बिया तुमचे नाही कामाचे
गुनचेरी राजाला नायसे बिया मिलत
मुगल राज्याला गेली आहा
नाय बिया विचाराया तुमाला त्याच्यासी बिया पायजेत होती
आमापाय बिया आहात
वान्याच्या दारी जाय जा कोरा रूमाल आनजा
मग नागलीचे बिया भेटली आद्य
वरीच्या तरीच्या डांगीच्या कुडाच्या
कोलब्याच्या घेतल्या आद्य निघून चालाया लागली आहा
बिया माडी माहता घिन गेली आहा
गाईचा गोरा, विरखाचे (सांगाचे) बुडाला बांधला आहा
नाकाने फोडले आहा, विसनी घेतले आहा
नागराच्या नयान्या आपून सेतावरीया रहल्या आहा
हालसे डोंगरी, हलसाना, पाटची डोंगरी (पाती) आनाया जायजा
लवनग्या सुतार बोलावला, कुलब्याला कुसा, लोहाराचे दारी,
लोहार दादा तुजी कामा रहु दे मला कुसा तयार करून दिजोस
सेकडा दाम चुकवला चालाया लागला आहे
चला जाऊ नागरा जूपाया, जा कोठी होलावर
परयानया कराया एक टक्का परयाना केल्या आहा
सेतीवरा पेरयून रिकामी झाली आहा,
ये होला डखलाया लागली आहा, तस्या होलत उखलून
रिकामी चला जाव माडी माहलात
जाव आपून नागर मागाया सात दिसाचे पेरयान्या झाल्या होत्या

ते हुन भात वाढाया दोन पाना वादून
चार पाना वादून पाच पाना वादून आली आहा
कुलबी लागले बोलाया,पानी नाही सोना पाडा
जामबेटीचे चिखल करजा भात खनाया लागली आहा
कुलबी लागली आहा खनाया
माठ भाजीचा मडा सात माडा घेतली आहा
सिडाच्या सहरात सात माडा घेतल्या आहे
पहली होती रावकरीन, मगा आली मालात आता झाली
मालकरी
एके काली दोन काडवा वादून दिजोस
एक थोबी, दोन थोबी दिजोस,
माल कोलीयास जायजोस,
दोघा कुलबी आवून हातात खुडतोस
हातात खुडतोस नको वाडती होयजोस
जसा कलनिया समीदर वादून आला
तसे तु तर वादून यीजोस
तसे आंबूना रीकामी झाली आहा
अखाड महिना वरतून गेला सरावन उगवता
सरावन वरतून गेला भादवा महीना उगुन आला
भाता होती गरबी झाली ते भाता निसवून पडली
खालच्या मार्गाला आनली आहा
हिवान महनी नाही खाती पसंत
झाली तांबड माती निघून गेली
नाही खाती चिंता मनी मुरूम मालीला निघून गेली
नाही खाली पसंत झाली उदार मानेला
तथ खात्री पसंत केली, अथ खला फार बरा उदार आहे
सातसे कमारीला हाका मारल्या
चला कमारी हो, खली खुरपा
खाल पासून खुरपाया लागली आहां
एकाच दिसाला खला खुरूप रिकामी झाली आहा
गायीची सीना केली आहा सारवन केला आहा

आता भाता कापाया लागली आहा
उडवीयावर उडवा, उडवाचे वर भरजोस,
भाता रिकामी झाले
पुस महना उगवला आहे, लोटीयाचे दुकानी अगरबत्ती
पुजाया आनजोस,
नारलाचे पुजाया आनजोस
तेवहु पुजा घेतली आहे
मडी माहली गेला आहे
भगताला अथ शरवून बिया तु कोठ जास
सानचे पाहराला आला आहे, वाडे सत
बसला आहे तंबाखू घेतली आहा
विडया वालल्या आहा
विडया तानले आहा
विडया तोडल्या आहा
हात घोबले आहा. पाय धोबले आहा
बारा जन वाडीत जान, खांबासी (खाभाडीसी) बसला
आहा
पांगलायाचे नावाचे कुडल ठेवले आहा
उडवेसी दादा तसी, ओडून वाडली आहे
खांबापासी नेली आहे
जागेवर डावे पायाचे घेतले आहे
पहल्या धडया सिलकीत खांडी करजोस
भारेला मुडा नाकरजोस
असी ही हालपेत नसी वाडेल होयजोस
तू जसा दुरूग वाढून झाला तसा पांगलाय वाढुन मी जोस
नारलीच्या वाडीत चाडत्वीया होती उसाचे वयात
चालती होती धानीच्या मुलाच्या खाडीचे कोल्हाचा
दोडकीयाच्या
वाडयात चांगल्या होत्या
मांडे पायेसी, पाय मुद्दल, आणि कोपरा पासी हात मुद्दल
तुझे करीता जीव मारून
अजगीना दगा फटका करजा नको

कुलबीला सुठी दिजोस
या दडा दुपालल्या मंगा चारी खंडाला जोघरल्या मंगा
धडा खांबेत भरली आहे
मलनी सुरूवात झाली झोडनी सुरूवात
मग भाताचा तांगड भरायाचा
धानाच्या गुनी लसनाच्या गुनी भरायच्या
या मलण्या चालल्या आहात
ढिगा कुलबी केली सहराला,
धानाच्या मुलीच्या च
ऊसाच्या काठया त्या घेतल्या आहा
केंलीचे लोगज्या घेतली आहा
गेली निघून सोटीचे दुकानावर गेली आहा
टिटकी बांगडी काली गाठी आईचा सामान घ्यायाला गावती
दिवा लावाया कडवा तेल गोडातेल घेतला आहे
लोटे मार्गे बारी वानी वर निघून आली
आता निघून तर भगत आला आहे
आईचा उपास वो दोघा कुलबी रहली आहा
सानच्या पाहराला निघून कनसरी माता (पांगलाय)
रेसमा कुमार झलती काजला कुमार जलती केली
केली महुवरी कोवा घेतला आहे
नारन देव हिरोबादेव महुवारी कोवा घेतला आहे
निघून वर चालल्या संजान (गावाला) सहराला
बोरेडत शहराला रानीचे पडवीयाला कोणी वार गेला काय
काला–काली हाताला तुली होती पायाला नेवरी होती
कालोच्या लोटनात मीलोच्या पुरज्यातीच्या मुखडाचा असाद केल्या होत्या
धावलाच पांगली केल्या, तसे बोरडे सहरासी
डहानू सहराला हीरोबा देव मुरूंबाबा वांजवत जाय

नारन देव मोडा–मोडे नाचत जाय
तसी पागलाय सदमा देव सदमा करून
रागाचे रात्री कुलल्याची पाठ सोडून जाया लागली
कुलबी होता हालात पडला
तुजी दसा फार दुर गेली आहे
वानगाव शहर, हिरोबा देव मार्गाला लागला
नारन पो आयेला मानपाया जात आहे
तरी पण तुझेवर हाय–हाय कुलब्या
नाभू (भिऊ नको) नाको भीजो
सनी बोलता पत्करल्या
नाभो मर्दा तुझी दसा फार दूर गेली आहे जात आहा
म्हणून तुझे करता जिव मार, जिवतार, उपास कर
गायीचा गोरा कुटून मार
दोन गोठावा धरती तोडली, धरतीचा पानी केला
असे तुझी हाल अर कसा केला रिन केला धीन केल
पालघर सहराला आईचा पता नाही लागत आहे
केल्वे सहराला केलीचे पाटीला दसावी हिडत होती
धर बाई केलीचे लोगरा दिन तुझे केली
दिन तुझे केली नाय धीन दासा पलाली आहे
दादर शहराला हिंडत जायीन ठाने सहराला
उजवी कालाली हुमयदेवीचे निघून गेली
तेथ हिमाय देव बोलाया लागली
तुझा तांगड मला दिजो तांगड चालाया लागला आहे
तुझी दासा वारोली शहराला

तेथे तांगडनी निया लागली आहा
रेम भरमबे गेली धिन नांगर हि दासा नागवी आहे
तुझी दसा पालवली काली गाठी अगलीत आहे
डाव्या हातात बांगडया आहात त्यावर तू हात टाकजोस
नाय नेयाची मला लाथन, मारला आहे.
सुपाखल भारला आहे. माझा कान तुटला आहा

मुसला खत मारल आहा. माझ दात पाडले आहे
भारी खल मारले आहा माझा हात तोडले आहा
भारारवाल तोडला आहा; शोडली तोडले आहा
मग हिरवा देव माझ्यावरी हवा, वाजवाया लागला आहे
तसी आमाल पांगलाय (पांगलआई) मानवली आहे
तसी घांगली बाजाया तयार झाला
गोनी वंजारा सातसे गोनी तयार करजो
सर्व वंजारा सिवे वंजारा तेहे वजारा
गोनी भराया केली च्या गोनी, नारलाच्या गोनी धनिया गोनी
भराया लागल्या
हाके वजार बारे वंजारा तांगड भर
सातसे तांगड भराया लागल्या
आयेच्या तांगड राम भरबी
तसी पांगलाय आईचे तांगड आनन्यान्या दादा
माझा कुनबी हातात पडल
चाकरी करल उघडा पानी पडत नाही
चल बाय फार बरा तुझा कुलबी सेवा करत आहा
आईच्या तांगडात बसली आहा रेमभरोमबी (देवता)
करनाली शहराला आला तांगड रेमभरोमबी
त्याच्या गालयाला भरम भोवाचा देव
आडवा फिरला नांगत आईची दसा
जात आहे तुझा बाय. जानाईना कोठ पडला
मी जाय कोसबाड गावात माझा कुलबी हालात आहे
वर्सा कुरावत कराया जात आहे
मेलेचा जिता करत, थोल्याचा धडा करन
तसा तांगड वालत आन
मागत मांगत घेऊन येत पांदे नाडनाड घेत येत
तसा तांगड सात समीद आडवा पडला
टाके दादाला हाका मारल्या
टाके दादा तारन आनजोस
माझा तांगड देवाऊन दिजोस
ये तास देवासन दिजोस

हे तारू देवारून दिजोस
रोकड दोन दिल्या चुकून
हाके वंजारा बोम्बे वजारा, बोबा ठोक
तसा तागड देवा लागला
सावटे सहरी मागे नड (जात) पनडे नाद पाड घेत जात
आयी माझे रे भरोसी थोमी थोमी
आयेचा तांगड रमी–चांद माता आडवी पडली
उभा केली ही पागल आहे जाता येता कोठे पडली
तलवाली शहराली आलत तसा तांगड वेच कालाला
तसा तांगड रेमभरोबी
कुलबी जगसुज झाली तुझा तांगड येत आहे
तांगड देवाये लोहे मार्गे
घाते कर सहरात निघून आला
मोरी तांदोबा आडवा पडला
येही सदमा केली–चावलाचा घागत केला
कोसलयाचा पुवार केला निलीसीचा पण केला
ये कोडीचा पुज केला
मुरवाच्या असाऱ्या केल्या आहा
माझा कुलबी माझी सेवा करा का नाही?
सदमा करून मी जात आहे
तसी सोसत लोहे मार्गे हाके वंजारा बोबे वंजारा
बोंबा मारत आहा तारपे वंजारा बोबे वंजारा
बोंबा मारत आहा. तारपे वंजार धागरे वंजारा
तांगड रेम भरी मबी रहन हआन
तसा देवाया लागला
बोरोडे शहरासी देवाया लागला
गावचा देव आडवा पडला
तेथे तांगड उभा केला दादा पांगलाय
पायनीचा पान केला वार्सीग पैनीचा बासीग केली
तनोडा सती झाले सपती झाले
कोसबाड गावात दिदोले होलात तांगड आला पुजीचे
होलात.

हाय. हाय कुजल्या भाजो नाभू मर्दा नको भीजो
सनी बुधला पाथरला खुलनाचे ढिगारी
खल्याचे तागड झाला ये तांगड कुलबीला थेपालन
हिडा
त्याच्या मग रासी केल्या
दोडकीच्या वडया कोहल्याच्या वडया
उसाच्या पडया चांज्पा केल्या
धनाच्या चांज्पा केल्या
हलदीच्या बडीया आयाचा लग्न
नाचोली पाना झाली
तसी मगा रेमभरोबी ठेपो–ठेपी बागान भावे खाली
लागले
ये तांगड वाडता करून
मेलीचा धजा करून थोटी चाजि तन करून
बारा आरवती कोंबडी पूजा केली
सोनी आडल्या कुलबीन आग हो केली
बारावाडीला आज सुबी दिजोस
ये कुलबीला सुटी दिजोस
सगलयांची पिन्याची दगा–फटका काही करजीस नको
वरजी पाउस पुरावा करजोस

☆ ☆ ☆ ☆

APPENDIX-4.1

पद आता जन्मा याचा, पुरुसा (पुरुष) दोन जेवनारादंत
चुल पेटल आता तु खा आनी मला पन दे
मी मोठा देव चुल पेटवत नाही आग फुकून तर
माझ्या मिस्या पेटतील वेडा बागडा तु चुल पेठव
आनी जेवना रांदता चुल पेटवल्या आनी जेवना
रांदली
पांच दिवसाचा पदर होता तो मावलून गेला
ताब्यात धड घेतला राजबावीला निघून गेली
कासर मानिला निघून गेली माती नांगाया
माती पसंत नाही झाली चीकून माती वलली
खनन्या केल्या मात्या काढल्या
खोली माती नेन तर मला बार होईल
आनी खोत्या असा कान होती
दुदीत मात्या नेईन तर दुघा असा पोट होईल
मगा चालाया लागली पलसाच्या बुडासी निघून गेली
तेथे विराल सोडून ठेवला, पलसाची फुला तांबडी झाली
सावरीच्या बुडासी निघून गेली
तथ विटाल सोडून ठेवली सावरीच फुला तांबडी झाली
ओडयाच्या वेलीसी निघून गेली. त्याची फुला रानी झाली
वाहती गंगाला निघून गेली मुरीआडे पानी गेली
गीरबीची चोली घारीला ठेवली. देवान साडी घारीला
ठेवली
माज्या ओडीत पान्यात गेली मज्या भिजवल्या
माथी भिजवल्या माथी बुडवत्था माजी चोलली
पदर वाहत्या गंगेत सोडून ठेवला. मुसाचा मसाला
पदर झेलून घेतला
ओली सोडली कोरडी लावली राजबावीला निघून गेली
घड चोलला मलला पानी भरला लोहटे मागी मज
माहली

घर आली अगरी निगरी भाजा केली पुरुसाला हाका
मारल्या
सोनिताटी जेवता वाढली देवान जेवन वाढला मग
मुखी मलला
सोडला घासाला जेवाला बसला
अंधेरी खोली निघून गेला. सोनेरी पलगा निजला
अंधेरी रानचे चडावडी करू लागला. नार होती गोंधलून
गेली
जेवन नाय भाव पानी नाय भाव, पोटीचा बामन आला
बोलू लागला, तुझ्या पोटात गरब आहे
गरभ वाडू लागला एक महिना झाला
दोन, तीन,....नव महिनी झाले
नव वेला नव दिस नव घटका नव तास
पोट दुःखु लागला.....
ईहुला हावका मारल्या लोटयाच्या दुकानात गेला
बारा सुया घेतल्या गजराईच्या हातात दिल्या
तु वर धदा सुडका काय सिवाय आनलास
सेवटी सहराला निघून गेला सुई आली
हातात घेतली लाकडी सुईन बारा बेरोटी झाली
गायीचे गोठनी निघून गेली. गाय गाबत होती
वेधू लागली डोकरे माझा कर
तुझ्या सिंगा काडसी तर सिंगा मारसी
पाया काडसी तर पायान मारसील
तुझा बालतुच सिंदजोस. धरती पाडजोस
चाटुन चुंबून चालता करजोस
मडी माहली निघून गेली. उखरडी ढीगावर कोंबडी चरत
होती
ती बोलाया लागली डोकरी जास कोठ?
एकाची दोघा कराया जाय
कोंबलीला बोलू लागली. तुझ्या पोटीला
हाड जन्मत घरात गेली बाई पडून होती

पोटात दुखत होवा तलाला तेल लावला
आडवा बाल चांगला गेला. बाई बालातन झाली
धरती वर बाल पडला नाल बांधली कच्च्या सुतावर
बोरधाची साली काढली नाल कापला वर दातली
देव धरती वर पडला

APPENDIX-5.1

महादेव गंगा गौरी उठाली सकालचे पाहरी
असा तु माझे आमचे भारजा
तार मालावर चल
आनि घोसाव्या भाताचा भात पाड
उखलावर नेऊन काड
सडीक चाऊल कांडून दे
अता घुंटीला (घरटीला) नेऊन पिठ दलवून मला दे.
आता महादेवाच्या हातात पीठ दिलां.
तांब्या भर पानी दिला
महादेवाने पिठ कालवून उन्डा वालला
त्याची महादेव गाय कराया लागला
सात गायी केल्या पिठाच्या
नाक, तोंड चार–पाय केला
शेपटी केली खांद केला डोले केला.
सात गायीनी पावल्या
कोरा सेला आनला आनी
आनल्या जातिला गायी होत्या सात
कोन्या सेल्याने झाकुन ठेवल्या
कासी तरी देवाची विधी होती
ती सोडली
मुरूद पानी (शुद्ध पाणी) गायीवर सांडला
गायीला सकी वती आली
गाय जिवंत झाली. चालती झाली महादेवाने हातीं
काठी घेतली
देव होता तो गायीचा गोवारी झाला
गायी चाराया नेल्या
रोडे मानेला नेल्या
तेथून वालल्या
कसोर मानेला
चरत–चरत खानगार डोंगराला नेल्या
बतीस उन्डे नेले

सात राती सहा दिवस राहल्या जंगलाला
तिकडसी देवान गायी वालल्या
दुपारी भरल्या
हेंबोरनीचा झाड होता
ती या झाडा खाली गायी गोठल्या
गायी मोजाया लागल्या
साहाच झाल्या गायी
गायीला गायी नाही तर गवसाया जातो आवासी
जायला नकोस
गायी गवसून देव हं ला
पण त्याला गायी काही गवसत नाही
देवाला पोटी भूक लागली
होटी तहान लागली
गंगा–गंगा साथ होती पान वाहीत होती
देवाना माडी वालून पानी पिला
देव मगा तया गंगेला चालाया लागला
तथ ऊगीसी झल होती
त्याला गाय धुतलाला होती ती
गाय मेलेली होती
तिच्या मुखासी पानी निघाला होता
देवान नागला होता ते पानी मी ही पिला
मग माइयावर आता जात पडली
गाय मरते खंडाला सावय केली (बाजूला)
मग देव निघून गेला
गायी होत्या तय तथ.
त्या साहा गायी हाकलल्या
चरत–चरत त्याच्या घरी घेऊन गेला
गोठीत गायी बांधल्या गायीच्या गोठीत देव बसला
त्याची भातारी त्याला बोलाया लागली की
गायीच्या गोठी बसून नको दूध ये
तो गोठीत बसून पडला
बाई बोलाव तरी तो उठत नाही

आता माझ्यावर जाती पढलीया
गायी मरून गेली
तीच्या मुखाचे पानी पिल्यावर जाता पडल्या
मी त्याला हात धरत नाही
जेवन–पानी मला वाढून धावा
खाऊन–पिऊन तो निघून गेला
राती वरतून गेल्या
सकालच्या पाहरी उठला
फिरून त्याच्या भारजाला बोलू लागला
आता देवाला बोसवायचा
बहरमदेव बोलवला नारन देव बोलवला
देवाचा महाल भरता देव बोलाया लागले
आता बहरम देवा तू ऊठ
मुकूठाची काठी–जातीची काठी घे
त्यांना तय घाट भरला (सेंदूर सोडून)
चावलाच्या पुंजलया ठेवल्या
त्यावर बारीक सा मडका आनला
त्यात पानी ठेवला, तिच्यावर कोरा सेला घातला
त्याच्यावर देवाला हात ठेवाये सांगला
बहरम देव मुठाची काठी घेऊन उठला
देवाला बोलाया लागला
आता देवान पानी पिलाय आहे
जात पडली आहे. याची गावली बोलायची आहे
तूमी देवहो आयकून घ्या
देव बोलत आहे. हातामध्ये काठी होती
एक भाल होती. पानी उडवत होता चारी बाजूला
तथ देव गाठी बोलत होता
सत गावठी सताची असी वावढी भानोजी
बीस सत ऐके देव फिरत होता
सत गावठी संताची आशा बोलत होता
बोलत होता भीस
आता पंच लोका हो देवाची जात झाली

तु मी बोला झाली
ध्वता तसा बोला नाय हवी तर तसा बोला
देवात पानी पिला, त्याची जात झाल
आता माझी चूकला तर
असां जात पाठावी. आता से गावठी बोलावी
जाते करून घ्यावी

APPENDIX-6.1

एके टाटीचा होता जेवनाला बसा, पर जाती होना ते उठून
बाजूला व्हा आज आमाला मानस्वा त्याची जात करायची
आहे
कासीचा बामन आला आहे, तो जेवायासाठी बोलला आहे
आता सगलेला हुकूल दिला, जेवा आता
पार्वती तू घरा राहतोस
ताहनेचा येल त्याला पानी दिजो
भूकेचे त्याला खाना
आम्ही जात आहा दुन्या नागाया
सगला वाडू लागला धरतीला बाहार लागला
गायीचा गो–हान टाकून लागला, कोंबडा बया कराया
लागला
असा भार मला नाही समा बर, मायीचा गोहान टापरी
मारली त आजगी धरतरी फुडून लागला
जाय आवा मी मरन कराया
माहादेव दादासी जाय मरन करया,
रडत–झडत जात होती, रडत गेली दारासी
दादा कोठ गेला आहे
दादास गेले दुन्या नागाया, गंगा गौरी सी
तू ज्या रडस?
तहान लागली हवी त पानी दिन
भूक लागली हवी त खाना दिन
पन दादास नाही वर माघारी वालीव
माधारी पलून फिरून रडत जात होती
तेथ गायीच्या गाठेनी होत्या
तेथे होता हिसाब पांडू,
भूंकु पाडू अर्जून पांडू होते
त्याच्या गायी गोठवीलया होत्या
तिथ विडा हाती होता
तिसी खेलता खेलत
धरती रडत झूरत गेली होवी

फूये ते कोठे जाते होती
वि गेली होती दादासी
दादा घरी मिल नाही?
क्या गेले होतीस?
त मरन कराया गेली होती,
जाता येता कराया गेली होती
फूये रांगये न मला सांग मी
मी बहरा आहे. मला कानात एकू येत नाही
रांगच गेली बोलाया लागली
मी जाता–येता मरन कराया गेली होती
त्याला राग आला हाताला धरता
फिरवले ना झोगून दिली
गोल कंकारे झूगारून दिली
तथ रडत होती।
तिकडसी महादेवा गंगा गौरी वलली होती दुन्या फिरून
गंगा–गौरी महादेवाला बोलाया लागली
गोल कंकारी कोनीतरी झूनत आहे
आपन नांगाया जाव
नागायला तर धरती बाय आहे
तूला धरती काय झाला?
सु:ख हवा न दु:ख तुझा,
ना दु:ख हवा त सु:ख करू
माता काम आहे, मला जाता–येता मरण कराया आहे
मला नाय सगावेन
हाताला धरला न उठवली
तुझे माहाली चल तुला जाता–येवा मरन,
आम्ही मरन करून देईन
तेथे गंगा गेल्यावर देवा गेली
मग इसा देवान माहला भरली
खंडून खंडाचा पिडा सिवला
राजून–राज्याचा खडून खंडाचा

एक बिडा आहे तो मानाचा सिवला
सगला विडा परातीत ठेवले
देवाला हाका मारल्या
देव रांगून गेले
राजा होती ती देवाने घेतली
खंडून–खंडा घेतली.

✯ ✯ ✯ ✯

राजा घेऊन (ज्याची–त्याची रजा घेतली)
देव गप्प रहत
एक विडा रहताय, एक राज राहलाय
वाटायच
वाटुन तुमाला सुटी दिन असा देव बोलत होता
पांडू देव होता, त्याच्या होत्या दोन भाताज्या
पांडू देव सकाली उठून पारधीला जात होता
दुपारी भरल्या आणि परत आल्या.
त्याच्या दोघी भाताज्या बोलाया लागल्या
देवाने महला भरली, राजवट देऊन देवाची रजा घेतला
मग पांडू देव बोलाया लागला
एखाद राज तरी मी हू घीन
इस्वर महालाला गेला
पांडू देव मरनाचा विडा होता तो
पायाचे भोवरे मारून उजवा हात टाकला
तो विडा उचलला होता मरनाचा
अर्धे वाटेला जान ना फोडून नागजोस
सारे देवान (होती तवडेला) सुट्टी दिली
देव नागून गेलं, अर्धे वाटेला पांडू देव गेला
विडा फोडू लागला त्यात होती मरनाची चिट्ठी
विचार कराया लागला के आपून विडा उचलला, पण
बेस नाही
मरनाचा विडा आहे, आता याला काय करावा
त्याला डोका दुखाया लागला

तुझे देवा बहनीस आहे, तर काय विचार कराल
मरन नाय कराला,
पांडू देव विचार करीत होता
त्याच्या होत्या दोघी भारजा
दोघी भारजा लागल्या बोलायला
आहे देवा तुमची बहनीसा,
काय तरी विचार करजा
पांडू देव तर गेला नीघुन
राहत करीत होता
बांद बादोस्ती करीत होता
लागला बांदो जेथावा माहना
याची कामा लागली चालायाला
त्याची होती सती कहभरी
त्याचे होवे साथी नांगर
यादे मरदा, नागर हिंडवत होवे
हि त्याची कामर (कामवाली)
भात खनत होती
अर्पनाचे काम वरी चालजा होता
भाताज्या आवत होत्या, ना गोरात आवात होती
भाताज्या त खनत रे होत्या
आता मदी आवाया गेली
आता देवा आवाया र गेली
न साथी सागरा हिंडवत रे होती
चिखरा पाना करत रे होती
तीथ मदी आवता रे होती
भाताज्या आनता रे होत्या
पांडू देवा त गेला निघून
भाताज्याला सुटी दिली रे होती
नागरेला रे सुटी दिली होती
तथ आला बैलाचा गोवारी
मग देव लागला बोलाया
निला मर्दा लागला बोलायला

गोवारी हो तुम्ही जायजा घरा
आज त मी बैला सी रह
पांडू देव त बेलासी रहला
बैला वालत हिंड
होता धुन तो गायीचा गोरा
पांडू देवान कसा नागला
पांडू देव त गेला निघूनी
गायीच्या गोरीसी गेला निघून
गायीचा गोरा का रे हसला?
पांडू देव तर गेला फसून
हिमा देवी सी पाय येचे आहा
तुझे देवा मरना तीला
हिमा ही पायता कसा सुटन
तुझा पन त जिवडा नेती
गायीच्या गोरयान तो अकल सांगतो
मला पन तो अक्कल सांगतो
मेडे माहली जायजो निघून
तूझे महाली जायजो निघून
बेस मेडी तू वाढजो
एक खोली भावली ठेवजो
सात खोल्या तू ठेवजो
एक खोलीत मावली ठेवजो
साती ही खोल्या चांगल्या ठेवजो
तेथ तू, तो हाडूपा ठेवजो
हडू प्याला पाठी ठेवजो
तुझे घर ती गोसा आनजो
तुझे मघली गोसा आनजो
कोंबोडीचे मासा आन जो
तिथ सुरा तू आन जो
देवा तू ना दारू अना जो
दारू आनून तयार ठेवजी
लोरया सेडची घागरी आनजो

धागन्या आनून दोरीला बांधजो
माझे देवा पायीला बंदजोस.
तुच मर्दा तयार रहजोस.
मीच ते सांजुन पाहजो
घागन्पा मगा सांजुन पाहजो
हाती तू धनवट घिजो
मला तुझ्या संगाती जे वाढजो
खुरसी फन देवाल दिजो
देवा तू आता भास जो
डोंगरा जायी काय देखाय
गायीचा गोरा नाचून पडला
खुरस्या दादून, देवाला दिल्या
दादा हो तुम्ही आता भासा जा
जूमा सिवाय खुरसी भासले
देवाचे देखत पडल्या
पांडू देवा देखज फडला
टोडल्या पांडू लागला बोलाया
तिन सुरा आनलाय
पहिला सुरा तिन आनल्याय
भाकरीच्या भाज्या आनल्या
कोबंडीच्या भाज्या आनल्या
मगायीना दाखा आनल्या
योच देव तर फार चांगला
पांडू देव तर फार चांगला
जुमा शिवाय माग झुमंधला
चल देवा खोल्या नांगाया
तुझ्या खोल्या चल नांगाय।
निघून गेले मोवले खोल्याला
पांडू देव लागला बोलायला
अजून खोल्या र फार चांगल्या
सात खोल्या गेले र निघून
निघून ना गेले हडप्याचे वाले

जूमा सिवाय हाडापे हलव रे
हीच खोली फार चांगली
पहली होती तीला पाहुन
जुमा सिवाय टाकली कोंडून
जुमा पाय हडपी कोंडून

☆ ☆ ☆ ☆

GLOSSARY

Abir—a powder made out of flower petals
Ain—a plant
Akhad—month of July according to the traditional calander
Ambadi—a vegetable plant
Ambil—Preparation of bermented Jowar.
Adhuli—a measure
Buffalo—a buffalo
Baachka—A Bundle
Bachkna—A bite
Bachka Madeni—exposition of wedding gift
Badhavani—engagement
Bahramā—god Brahma
Baiyancha Khanda—narrative for women
Basinga—the wedding crown
Batasi—triangular entrance of the wedding pendal
Batala—tainted
Baras—a feast before divali - twelvth day before divali
Barik Mula—one of the rituals of the wedding ceremony
Bhagat—shaman
Bhagi—a part
Bhaji—vegetable
Bhakar—a millet bread
Bhakta—a devotee
Bhal—a spear
Bhutali—a witch
Bombil—a sea fish variety
Borru—a stick, also used for writing
Candravat—gods of moon
Chander-Surya—The sun and the moon
Chameli—a tree
Chapati—wheat roll.
Charvasi devi—a local goddess

Chauka—a pictoral depiction during the wedding on the wall
Chaukya—a guard post
Chaudas—The fourteenth day of the month
Chavli—a pulse
Chedd—poles for the sprits
Chitar—A painting
Cunji—a rice preparation
Dāb—a plant used during rituals of Dis.
Dagdi deva—the stone god
Dasi—A lady servant
Dhak—small drum
Dhaklya bhagat—the assistant to the shaman
Dangar—a vegetable (Pumpkin)
Darunga—a hillock
Dava—a Claim
Davli—pumpkin
Dayicha deva—a local god
Deni—a plant
Deve Chowk—Gods painted in a suare during marriage
Deva nach—emulation of the dance of the gods
Dez—gift before the marriage
Dhake bhagat—the one who plays the small drum
Dhänk—small musical instrument
Dharana kori— goddess
Dhomsī—Dhol
Dhavaleri—the marriage priestess
Dis—death ceremony
Dis Khand—the narrative narrated at the death ritual
Diva nangane—diagnosis
Dolak-—a drum
Dutari—a two strings musical instrument
Erandi—Caster oil
Fālli—wedding gift of a white cloth.
Fagawa—a gift given at the time of holi
Gal sut—necklace tied by groom around his brides neck.
Ganda—mad

Gāṭhi—necklace made in black beeds
Gavli-a—Chant
Gavri-baiya—Those who perform this dance.
Ghad—a pot
Ghangli Bhagat—The Bhagat who plays a musical instrument
Gharca Devā—Household gods
Gharor—the bridegroom staying at his in-laws
Ghat—a high place
Ghosal—a vegetable
Gohdī Chedda—The horse-god.
Gorada—a tree
Govari—a cowherd
Gulal—lead powder
Gungeri—wasp
Guru dakshina—offering to the teacher
Hafta—a regularised repayment
Halad—turmeric powder to be
Halp—applied during the wedding.
Himai—a warli goddess
Hirva deva—a warli god
Himai—a goddess
Jalavat—Halluncination
Jaat-Caste
Jaat khanda—a narration during the purification rite
Janvat—To remember
Johar—a greeting
Joli—a craddle, a birth ceremony
Kadia deva—God arred on ward
Kahali—shehenai, a musical instrument
Kakdia—cucumber
Kankar—pebbles
Kanis—ear of corn
Kardode—Fruit of a particular tree
Karvi—a plant
Kansari khand—story of the corn goddess
Khandara—Parts of a khand.

Khadi—a piee of mutton; To 'see the grain.'
Khandadiva—lamp lit for a particular khand.
Khanda—a narrative
Kharmadh—a pole at the threshing floor
Khurasani—oil seeds
Kiran mokla—rays of the sun
Kohala-red—Pumpkin
Makhari chedda—God of the village entrance
Nagari—city
Nagli—a type of grain
Namin—a form of greeting.
Nangar—plough
Nava—newly harvested rice
Nirmal deva—A clean god
Ottani—ओटी भरणे
Pada—hamlet
Padava—a festival before Divali
Paghavat—spread net
Pal—a tree variety
Palad—small hut in the field
Palicha khanda—a part of a major narrative
Pangal—lame
Pangaliaī—lame goddess
Panti—earthern lamp
Parnai—Invitatition for marriage
Pasoda—a colourful cloth
Pat formula—a form of marriage
Pavasa—rain
Pehurāvanī—wedding gift (cloth) given by Bridegroom/Bride by to relatives.
Phani—comb
Pidda—bad omen
Pitha—a depot
Phorsa—a type of snake
Punjalī—small heap of rice
Puniv—full moon

Rāas—a heap of paddy, also related to threshing
Raktimahal
Rān—forest
Ropni—transplantation
Revada—a mighty bird
Rui—a wild flower worn during marriage
Rupajal—Hot water
Sagpan deth—steam of the teak leaf
Salad deva—a deity
Sȧmidhar—the sea
Savasini—a married woman
Sarovar deva—lord of the stream
Sevali—a vegetable
Salad—basket in which the deities are kept
Sendoor—red lead powder
Sedghol—rice wap kept in the basked (Salad).
Shannibudia Sind—a bamboo preparation
Shimga—Holi feast
Shira—veins of the bettle leaf
Soni jal—golden water
Sudki—sari
Supari—bettle nut
Surya—the sun
Sutar—carpenter
Tangad—not made of two coconnuts
Tarpa—a musical instrument
Tika—mark given on the forehead
Torni chedda—a garland placed on two poles to avoid the evil spirits
Tokre—a clan
Ture—the band players
Ugari—the pot that collects the remains of the dead after cremation
Ukhad—pounding hole
Ukhali—a small ukhal

Umber—a wild fig tree
Ungavita baiga—a god facing the east.
Vad—banyan tree
Vadga madhar—a compound behind the horse
Vaghia deva—the tiger god
Vaina—rice preparation
Vani—the trader
Vanglava deva—a deity
Vara—the wind
Vari—pilgrimage
Vavdi—the whirl wind
Vida—bettle leaf
Valuk—cucumber
Vir deva—a god
Vigna devi—evil spirits
Waghoba deva—the god of the boundry
Zotinga Baman—A Guru
Zun bhagat—the one who gets possessed

BIBLIOGRAPHY

Boxer, C.R.—1969—*The Portuguese Seabourne Empire : 1415-1825*. Hutchinson and Co., London.

Carpentier—1933—*Jarl, Livro da Seita Dos Indios Orientais of Fatheer Jacob Fenicio*, Ed. and Introduction, Uppala, Almquist and Wiksells Boktrycheri.

Dalmia, Y.—1982—*The Painted world of The Warlis*, Lalit Kala Academy, New Delhi.

Gadgil, M. & R. Guha—1993—*This Fissured Land*, Oxford University Press, Oxford Melbourne.

Halmendroff V. F.—1943—*Chenchus : The Jungle Folk of the Deccan.* Macmillan, London

Naik, Chitra—1978—*Growing up at Kosbad Hill : A Study of the Vikaswadi Experiment*, Gram Bal Shikshan Kendra, Kosbad, Thane.

Paruleker, Godavari—1975—*Adivasi revolt : The Story of the Warli Peasant in Struggle*, National Book Agency, Calcutta.

Report of the Aboriginal Hill Tribes of the Partially Excluded Areas in the Province of Bombay, Government Central Press, Bombay, 1939.

Save, K. J.—1945—*Warlis*, Padma Publication Ltd., Bombay.

INDEX